INDUSTRIAL PHARMACY - II

IN ACCORDANCE WITH PCI SYLLABUS FOR B.PHARMACY

KOSIKA SANDEEP | VAKKALAGADDA RAVI KUMAR | KONDAPURAM PARMESHWAR

Copyright © Kosika Sandeep, Vakkalagadda Ravi Kumar, Kondapuram Parmeshwar
All Rights Reserved.

ISBN 979-888555318-6

This book has been published with all efforts taken to make the material error-free after the consent of the author. However, the author and the publisher do not assume and hereby disclaim any liability to any party for any loss, damage, or disruption caused by errors or omissions, whether such errors or omissions result from negligence, accident, or any other cause.

While every effort has been made to avoid any mistake or omission, this publication is being sold on the condition and understanding that neither the author nor the publishers or printers would be liable in any manner to any person by reason of any mistake or omission in this publication or for any action taken or omitted to be taken or advice rendered or accepted on the basis of this work. For any defect in printing or binding the publishers will be liable only to replace the defective copy by another copy of this work then available.

Contents

CHAPTER I

PILOT PLANT SCALE UP TECHNIQUES

INTRODUCTION:

- The Pilot plant is a Hybrid Development facility and Manufacturing unit, which integrates followings;
    - Development,
    - Early development activities,
    - Clinical supply manufacture,
    - Technology evaluation,
    - Scale up and
    - Transfer to production sites,
- A ***pilot plant*** can also be defined as the pre-commercial production system which includes new production technology and produces small volumes of new technology-based products (Fig 1).
- ***Scale-up*** is the process of increasing the batch size or a procedure for applying the same process to different output volumes.
- The Pilot plant studies must include;
    - Current Good Manufacturing Practices (cGMP) environment,
    - Highly trained and skilled staffs,
    - Equipment support,
    - Facility of through and close examination of the formula.
- The factors that must be determine for successful product scale up are;
    - The requirements,
    - Training,
    - The reporting relationships,
    - Responsibility of personnel.

- The pilot plant, production and process control must be evaluated, validated and finalized during the scale up.
- The pilot plantplays an important role in the technology evaluation, scale up and transfer activities of new products.

Pilot plant scale up activities:

- The *major activities* takes place during scale up in early development phase are;
  - Technical aspects of process development,
  - Technical aspects of scale up,
  - Organisation responsibility
  - Determination of responsibility of technology transfer team,
  - Technology transfer documentation,
  - FDA pre-approval inspection preparation.

Major technical aspects:

- The scale up of pilot plant includes *major technical aspects* that are;
  - In early development,
    - Identification of critical components,
    - Control of critical components,
    - Identification of formulation variables,
    - Control of formulation variables,
- Simulating the pilot plant equipment with manufacturing areas equipment.
- Identification of critical process parameters.
- Identification of operating ranges for the pilot plant equipment
- Collection of data of Product and process.

Objectives of Pilot plant scale up:

- Avoidance of the problems associated with the scale-up.
- Production and process controls guidelines preparation.
- To identify the critical features of the process
- Preparation and providing of Master Manufacturing Formula for manufacturing.
- Evaluation and Validation for process and equipment.
- Examination of the formula to assess the batch stability.

Significance of Pilot Plant:

- Standardization of formulae.
- Review of range of relevant processing equipment.
- Optimization and control of production rate.
- Information on infrastructure of equipment during the scale up batches.
- Information of batches physical space required for equipment.
- Identification of critical features to maintain quality of a product.
- Appropriate records and reports to support GMP.

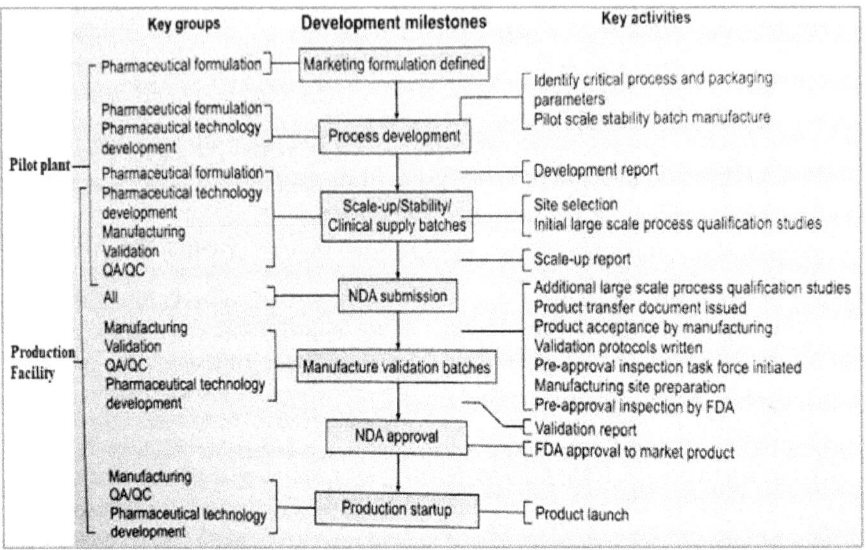

Enter CaptionFig 1. The layout of the relationship between different activities during technology transfers from the pilot plant to the production facility.

Reporting Responsibility:

- The objective of the reporting responsibility in Pilot plant is to facilitate the transfer of a product from the laboratory into production.
- The effectiveness of Pilot plant is determined by the ease with which the new product or process is brought into routine production.
- This could be possible if a good relationship exists between the pilot plant group with other groups (Research & Development, Processing, Packaging, Engineering, Quality Assurance, Quality Control, Regulatory and Packaging) of the company.
- The formulator who developed the product can take the product into the production.
- The formulator continues to provide the support to the other departments even after the transition into the production has been completed.

Personnel requirements:

- The Qualification required for a person to work in pilot plant organization are;
    - Good theoretical knowledge on blending
    - Pharmaceutical industry experiences.
    - Ability to develop good relationships with other personnel.
    - Good communication skill (Writing and speaking).
    - Practical Experiences in production areas about formulation, process and equipment.
    - Should be able to understand the intent of the formulator and perspective of production personnel.
    - Must have minimum knowledge on Engineering, Electronic and Computer.
    - Must have knowledge on Physical, Chemical, Biochemical and Medical attributes of dosage form.
    - Must be aware on the principle of GMP Practices.
- The individual responsibilities should be clearly understood by the individuals, which must be recorded.

Space requirements:

The space required in pilot plant is divided into 4 areas that are as follows;

- Administration and information area:
    - Adequate office and desk space should be provided for both scientists and technicians.
    - The space should be adjacent to the working area.
- Physical testing area:

- This area should provide permanent bench top space for routinely used physical- testing equipment.

- Standard equipment and floor space:

  - The sufficient specified space must be there for free installation, operation and easy maintenance of the equipment.

- Storage area:

  - Storage area for in process materials, finished bulk products, retained samples, experimental production batches, packaging materials (segregated into approved and unapproved areas).

  - Controlled environment space allocated for storage of stability samples.
  - Separate provisions for API and excipients further segregated into approved and unapproved areas according to GMP.

Training:

- The various departments that are responsible for compliance of GMP are;

  - Engineering
  - Quality control
  - Material handling
  - Warehousing and distribution
  - Purchasing.

- Depending on complexity of the job, each person involved in manufacturing, Processing, packaging and holding of a drug product, must receive the GMP and other specific training.
- The employee those need training are divided into the following categories;

- New employees.
- Those employees who are assigned with a new job.
- Those employee whose performance a task falls below required standard.

The employee get trained on following activities as per the GMP and FDA guidelines that are;

- Technical environment
- Dealing with potent or dangerous chemicals
- Working with system of weights and measures
- Checking of manufacturing steps, containers, equipment and drying racks.
- Identification of packaging.
- Proper stock rotation system.
- Raw material inspection.
- Quality validation.

Review of the Formula:

- The objective of each ingredient and its contribution to the final product manufactured on small scale equipment must be thoroughly understood.
- The modification in formulation during the scale up is possible to be done in phase III trial, so that sufficient time could be available for generation of meaningful long term stability data in support of a proposed New Drug Application (NDA).

Raw materials:

- One major responsibility of a Pilot plant is the approval and validation of active and excipient raw materials used in the Pharmaceutical products.
- This is because the raw materials used during the small scale formulation trials may not be representative of the large volume shipment of material due to change in raw materials properties like particle size, shape,

morphology, bulk density, static charges, rate of solubility, flow property and colour.

- An alternative supplier must be arranged as stand by basis which must validate the batches for manufactured products.

Relevant Processing Equipment:

- The selection criteria for one equipment to produce effective product within the proposed specifications are equipment must be economic, simple (In installation, handling, cleaning and maintenance), efficient and most capable of consistently producing a product.
- The size of the equipment should be such that experimental trials can be run that are meaningful and relevant to the production sized batches.

Production Rate:

- For determination of production rate, size and type of equipment required, the immediate and future market requirement must be considered.
- The selection of process and equipment to produce batches at a frequency need following considerations that are;
    - The time required to clean the equipment between the batches.
    - The product loss in the equipment during the manufacture.
    - The number of batches that need to be tested before release of product.

Process Evaluation:

- Things that should be critically examined during the Process Evaluation are;

- Order of addition of the components including adjustment of their amount.
- Mixing speed ant time.
- Rate addition of granulating agent, solvents and drug solutions.
- Heating and cooling rates.
- Filter size for liquids.
- Type and nature of filter media used for liquids.
- Screening size for solids.
- Drying temperature and time.
- Fan speed.

- The basis for process optimization and validation is the knowledge on effect of above mentioned parameters on the in process and finished product quality.
- The objective of process validation to ensure the selected process could be able to produce quality products at various critical stages of production.
- This is possible by critically monitoring the within the batch variation of measurable parameters like content uniformity, moisture content and compressibility.
- Some measurable change in the materials may take place during the processes like milling, mixing, heating, cooling, drying, sterilizing, compacting and filling, should be evaluated.
- The process remains validated only if there is no change in the formula, quality of the ingredients and equipment configuration.
- The manufacturing process and quality control information should be reviewed on an annual basis and should be followed by re-validation to ensure that changes have not occurred.

Preparation of Master Manufacturing Procedure:

The Master Manufacturing Procedure includes followings;

- The Process or Manufacturing Direction.

    - Process direction should be precise and explicit.

  - Must be written in a simple manner which should be easily understood by the operator.

- The Chemical Weight Sheet.

  - Identification of chemical required.
  - Quantities of chemical to be added.
  - Order of chemicals to be added.
  - The name and Identification number of the ingredient must be mentioned.

- The Sampling Direction.

  - Time of sampling of finished product.
  - Manner of sampling of finished products.

- The Batch record direction.

  - The batch record directions should include specification for addition rates, mixing times, mixing speeds, heating and cooling rates and temperature.

- The In-Process Specification.

  - Must mention a simple and easy access specification for easy understanding of operators.

- The Finished Product Specification.

  - The drug in the dose specified.
  - The self-life of the product.
  - The capability of the process.
  - The reliability of the test methods.
  - The stability kinetics of the product.

The periodic revalidation, GMP and monitoring of finished product test results via control charts are essential to maintaining consistent product quality.

GMP Consideration:

- The check list of the GMP items that should be a part of the scale-up or new product or process introduction including following;
    - Equipment qualification.
    - Process Validation.
    - Regulatory schedule preventive maintenance.
    - Regular process review and revalidation.
    - Relevant writing standard operating procedures.
    - The use of competent, technically qualified personnel.
    - Adequate provision for training of personnel.
    - A well-defined technology transfer system.
    - Validated cleaning procedures.
    - Arrangement of material to avoid cross contamination.

Transfer of Analytical Methods to Quality Assurance:

- Analytical methods developed in research must be transferred to the QA department.
    - Transfer process includes the following aspects;
    - Review the process to make sure that the proper analytical instrument is available.
    - Personnel should be trained to perform the test.
    - Reliability of the test should be checked.
    - At last assay procedure should be reviewed before transfer

A. PILOT PLANT SCALE UP CONSIDERATIONS FOR SOLIDS:

- The following points to be carefully consider during scaling up the solid dosage forms;
    - Batch size from intermediate to large scale production.
    - Each stage of operation.
    - Different types of equipment.
    - Use of sophisticated instruments with larger volume load.
    - Various sizes of equipment.

Material Handling:

The handling of materials is quite different and necessary to handle carefully in medium and large scale production from the laboratory scale (Mostly poured by hand or scooped).

- The characteristics of materials like density, size, shape and static charge must be taken into consideration while adopting the processing steps like;
    - Lifting and tilting of drums,
    - Vacuum loading system,
    - Screw feeding systems,
    - Metering pump systems.
- Any material handling system must deliver the accurate amount of the ingredient to the destination.
- The cross contamination must be prevented if a system uses transfer of materials for more than one product step.
- This is accomplished by use of validated cleaning procedure for the equipment.

Chemical Weighing:

- The incorrect ingredients and quantities may lead to cross contamination and misbranded brand during chemical weighing.

- A central weighing department should have for all the processing areas due to following advantages;

  - Centralization of responsibility,
  - Avoidance of duplicating weighing facility,
  - Lower labour cost.

- A chemical weighing department should be designed to provide supervision, checkers, lightening, dust collection, adequate sanitation, proper weighing equipment, supply of sink and drain board, cabinets, vacuum supply system, printing scale facility and meters for liquids.
- For weighing of dye and high potent drugs, a separate room must be equipped.

Tablet blending and Granulation:

Blending and Granulation:

- Powders to be used for encapsulation or to be granulated must be well blended to ensure good drug distribution.
- Inadequate blending at this stage could result in discrete portions of the batch being either high or low in potency to avoid drug content variation.
- Steps should also be taken to ensure that all the ingredients are free of.
- The lumps and agglomerates can be removed by doing screening or milling of the ingredients should be done to avoid flow problems, non-reproducible compression and encapsulation process, to facilitate content uniformity of the product.
- In blending, segregation and mixing operation takes place which depends on particle size, shape, hardness and density.

Dry Blending and Direct Compression:

- Different blenders used in blending are V- blender, double cone blender, Ribbon blender, Slant coneblender, Bin blender, Orbiting screw blenders, vertical and horizontal high intensity mixers.

- The factors affect the optimization of blending operation of directly compressible materials are;

- The order of addition of components to the blender.
- The mixing speed – Planetary type mixer, Tumbling Mixer, Cone Type Mixer.
- The mixing time –It affects compressibility of Finished Material.
- The use of auxiliary dispersion equipment with the mixer – Use chopper cell in Twin Shell Mixer.
- The mixing action – Determined by the Mechanics of the Mixer.
- The blender loads Optimum working volume and normal working range.

Slugging (Dry Granulation):

- The dry powder cannot be compressed directly due to poor flow and compression properties.
- The slugging is done by using the Tablet Press of 15 tonnes.
- After compression, slugs are broken down by Hammer Mill with suitable particle size distribution.
- The granulation by dry compaction can also be achieved by passing powders between two roller which put pressure of 10 Tonnes per linear inch.

Wet Granulation:

- The most common reasons given to justify granulating are;

  - To impart good flow properties to the material,
  - To increase the apparent density of the powders,
  - To change the particle size distribution,

- Uniform dispersion of active ingredients.

- Traditionally, wet granulation has been carried out using Sigma blade mixer and Heavy-duty planetary mixer.
- Wet granulation can also be prepared using tumble blenders equipped with high-speed chopper blades.
- More recently, the use of multifunctional "processors" that are capable of performing all functions required to prepare a finished granulation, such as dry blending, wet granulation, drying, sizing and lubrication in a continuous process in a single equipment.
- The factors that affecting the Fluidized Bed Granulator are;

  - Process Inlet Air Temperature,
  - Atomization Air Pressure,
  - Air Volume,
  - Liquid Spray Rate,
  - Nozzle Position and Number of Spray Heads,
  - Product and Exhaust Air Temperature,
  - Filter Porosity.

Drying:

- The most common conventional method of drying a granulation continues to be the circulating hot air oven, which is heated by either steam or electricity.
- The important factors to consider as part of scale-up of an oven drying operation are airflow, air temperature, and the depth of the granulation on the trays.
- If the granulation bed is too deep or too dense, the drying process will be inefficient, and if soluble dyes are involved, migration of the dye to the surface of the granules.

- Drying times at specified temperatures and airflow rates must be established for each product, and for each particular oven load.
- Fluidized bed dryers are an attractive alternative to the circulating hot air ovens.

- The important factors considered as part of scale up fluidized bed dryer are optimum loads, rate of airflow, inlet air temperature and humidity.
- The parameters to be considered for drying process by using Tray Dryer for scale up areAir flow, Air temperature, Depth of the granulation on the trays, Monitoring of the drying process by the use of moisture and temperature probes and Drying times at specified temperatures and air flow rates for each product.
- The Parameters to be considered for the drying process by using a Fluid Bed Dryer for scale up are Optimumload, Air Flow Rate, Inlet Air Temperature and Humidity of the incoming air.

Reduction of Particle size:

- Compression factors that may be affected by the particle size distribution are flowability, compressibility, uniformity of tablet weight, content uniformity, tablet hardness, and tablet color uniformity.
- First step in this process is to determine the particle size distribution of granulation using a series of "stacked" sieves of decreasing mesh openings.
- Particle size reduction of the dried granulation of production size batches can be carried out by passing all the material through an oscillating granulator, a hammer mill, a mechanical sieving device, or in some cases, a screening device.
- As part of the scale-up of a milling or sieving operation, the lubricants and glidants, which in the laboratory are usually added directly to the final blend, are usually added to the dried granulation during the sizing operation.
- This is done because some of these additives, especially magnesium stearate, tend to agglomerate when added in large quantities to the granulation in a blender.

Facilities:

- To avoid cross contamination in scale up and to facilitate the cleaning of equipment effectively, following facilities must be available that are;

  - Presence of separate room with availability of more space,
  - Must have granulation as unit operation,
  - Must have washing and drainage facilities,
  - Must have cold, hot water and steam supply system,
  - Platform should be with stainless steel or non-dust material system,
  - Air condition system is encouraging but if absent, window must be screened,
  - Use of a multifunctional processing system.

Granulation Handling and Feed System:

- The handling of the finished granulation in the compression area is either by Hand scooping for small scale or by sophisticated automated handling system with vacuum or mechanical system for large scale.
- The properties of material like size, size distribution and flow property affects the tablet properties like drug content uniformity, tablet weight, thickness and hardness.
- For efficient cleaning, sophisticated material handling systems like long lengths transfer tubes, valves, vacuum and pneumatic pumps should be used.

Tablet Compression:

- The tablet press performs following functions during the compression are;

  - Filling of an empty die cavity with granulation.
  - Pre-compression of granulation.
  - Compression of granules.
  - Ejection of the tablet from the die cavity and take-off of the compressed tablet.

- The prolonged trial runs at press speeds is generally adopted to find out the potential compression problems like sticking to the punch surface, tablet hardness, capping, and weight variation detected.
- High-speed tablet compression depends on the ability of the press to interact with granulation.
- During selection of high speed press criteria that should be considered are;

    - Granulation feed rate.
    - Delivery system should not change the particle size distribution.
    - System should not cause segregation of coarse and fine particles.
    - It should induce static charges.

- The die feed system must be able to fill the die cavities adequately in the short period of time that the die is passing under the feed frame.
- The smaller the tablet, the more difficult it is to get a uniform to fill high press speeds.
- For high-speed machines, induced die feed systems with a variety of feed paddles and variable speed capabilities, are necessary.
- Compression of the granulation usually occurs as a single event as the heads of the punches pass over the lower and under the upper pressure rollers.
- This causes the punches to penetrate the die to a pre-set depth, compacting the granulation to the thickness of the gap set between the punches.
- The rapidity and dwell time in between this press event occurs is determined by the speed at which the press is rotating and by the size of compression rollers.
- Larger the compressions roller, the more gradually compression force is applied and released.
- Slowing down the press speed or using larger compression rollers can often reduce capping in a formulation.
- The final event is the ejection of compressed tablets from the die cavity.
- During compression, the granulation is compacted to form tablet, bonds within compressible material must be formed which results in sticking.
- High levels of lubricant or over blending can result in a soft tablet, decrease in wettability of the powder and an extension of the dissolution time.

- Binding to die walls can also be overcome by designing the die to be 0.001 to 0.005 inch wider at the upper portion than at the centre in order to relieve pressure during ejection.

Tablet Coating:

- Many changes in Sugar coating (Carried in conventional coating pans), due to new developments in coating technology (Conventional sugar coating pan changed to perforated pans or fluidized-bed coating columns), changes in safety and environmental regulations.
- The development of new polymeric materials has resulted in a change from aqueous sugar coating to aqueous film coating.
- The tablets must be sufficiently hard to withstand the tumbling to which they are subjected in either the coating pan or the coating column.
- Some tablet core materials are naturally hydrophobic, and in these cases, film coating with an aqueous system may require special formulation of the tablet core and/or the coating solution.
- A film coating solution may have been found to work well with a particular tablet in a small lab coating pan but may be totally unacceptable on a production scale.
- To facilitate the efficient coating the tablet should not be designed as flat surface or sharpe edges.

Encapsulation of Hard Gelatin Capsules:

- The High Speed equipment is used to prepare the capsule by using the processed powder blend with following particle characteristics like particle size distribution, bulk density, compressibility to promote good flow property.
- This facilitates the formation of compacts of the right size and of sufficient cohesiveness to be filled into capsule shells.
- Filling of capsule is done by two filling systems;
    - Zanasi or Martelli form slugs in a dosator.

- Hofliger-Karg Machine

- Weight variation in capsules may come due to poor flow characteristics, improper lubrication and plug sticking to the dosator plunger surface.
- Overlay lubrication may create problems in weight variation, disintegration, dissolution and Bioavailability.
- The characteristics of granulation and the finished products are greatly influenced by the type and size of equipment used for blending, granulating, drying, sizing and lubrication.
- For better encapsulation, need of controlled environmental conditions that are Controlled humidity (RH 45 to 55 %) system in processing and encapsulation (RH 35 to 65 %) room and appropriate temperature condition of 15 to 25 °C.

B. PILOT PLANT SCALE UP CONSIDERATIONS FOR LIQUID ORALS:

- The physical form of a drug product that can be incorporated demonstrates Newtonian or Pseudoplasticflow behaviour.
- It conforms to its container at room temperature.
- Liquid dosage forms may be dispersed systems or solutions.
- In dispersed systems there are two or more phases, where one phase is distributed in another.
- A solution refers to two or more substances mixed homogeneously.

Steps of liquid manufacturing process:

- Planning of material requirements.
- Liquid preparation.
- Filling and Packing.
- Quality assurance.

Critical aspects of liquid manufacturing

- Physical Plant.
- Heating, ventilation and air controlling system.

- The effect of long processing times at suboptimal temperatures should be considered in terms of consequences on the physical or chemical stability of ingredients as well as product.

Solution:

- The parameters to be considered are for scale up of solutions are;

  - Impeller diameter.
  - Tank size (diameter).
  - Number of impellers.
  - Impeller type.
  - Mixing capability of impeller.
  - Rotational speed of the impeller.
  - Height of the filled volume in the tank.
  - Number of baffles.
  - Transfer system.
  - Clearance between Impeller Blades and wall of the mixing tank.
  - Filtration equipment (should remove desired materials but should not remove active or adjuvant ingredients).
  - Passivation of Stainless Steel (Pre-reacting the SS with acetic acid or nitric acid solution to remove. the surface alkalinity of the Stainless Steel).

Suspension:

- The parameters to be considered are for scale up of suspension are;

- Versator (To avoid air entrapment).
- Wetting of suspending agent.
- Addition and dispersion of suspending agents.
- Selection of the equipment according to batch size.
- Time and temperature required for hydration of the suspending agent.
- Mixing speeds (High speed should not be used as it leads to air entrapment).
- Mesh size (Must be able to remove the foreign particulates and sieve selected based on production batch size trials).

Emulsion:

- The parameters to be considered are for scale up of emulsion are;
    - Homogenizing equipment.
    - Temperature.
    - Mixing equipment.
    - Phase densities.
    - In-process or final product filters.
    - Phase volumes.
    - Screens, pumps and filling equipment.
    - Phase viscosities.

C. PILOT PLANT SCALE UP CONSIDERATIONS FOR SEMI SOLIDS:

- The following parameters are to be considered during the scale up of semisolid products;
    - Mixing speed.
    - Mixing equipment (Could be able to move semisolid mass from outside walls to the centre and from bottom to top of the kettle).

- Motors (Drive mixing system with appropriate handling system at its most viscous stage).
- Heating and cooling process.
- Component homogenization.

- Product transfer.
- Addition of active ingredients.
- Working temperature range.
- Shear during handling and transfer from manufacturing to holding tank to filling lines.
- Transfer pumps (Easily must move viscous material without applying excessive shear and free of entrapped air).

- Following parameters must be consider during choosing the size and type of pump,
- Pumping rate.
- Pumping pressure required should be considered.
- Product compatibility with the pump surface.
- Product viscosity.

SUPAC (SCALE UP AND POSTAPPROVAL CHANGES) GUIDELINES:

- SUPAC represents the changes recommended by the US FDA at the time of scale up or approval of NDA / ANDA.
- In the process of developing a new drug product, the batch sizes used in the earliest human studies are small and the size of the batches is gradually increased (Scale-up).
- The scale-up process and the changes made after approval in the composition, manufacturing process, manufacturing equipment, and change of site have become known as Scale-Up and Post approval Changes, or SUPAC.

The SUPAC Guidelines define;

- The level of changes – Minor, Moderate and Major Changes.
- Test – Application test, *in vitro* dissolution and *in vivo*
- Filing – Annual report, changes being effected supplement and Prior Approval Supplement.
- The level of changes may impact on formulation and quality performance in following levels;
    - Level 1: unlikely to have detectable Impact.
    - Level 2: could have significant impact.
    - Level 3: likely to have significant impact.
- These guidelines provide recommendations for post approval changes in;
    - The components or composition change,
    - The site of manufacture change,
    - The scale-up of manufacture change
    - The manufacturing (process and equipment) change.

A. The components or composition changes:

- This section focuses on changes in excipients in the drug product.
- SUPAC-MR - Excipient critical or non-critical to the Modified drug release.
    - Changes in non-release and release controlling excipients.
- SUPAC-SS - Changes in preservative in semisolid formulations.
- SUPAC-IR Changes for immediate-release solid oral dosage forms.

B. The site changes of manufacture:

- Changes in location of the site of manufacture, packaging operations and/or analytical testing laboratory.
- Do not include any scale-up changes, changes in manufacturing (including process and/or equipment), or changes in components or composition.
- Current Good Manufacturing Practice (CGMP) inspection.

Level I Changes -

Classification-Single facility where the same equipment, standard operating procedures (SOP's), environmental conditions (e.g., Temperature and humidity) and controls, and personnel common. Test Documentation-Application/ compendia requirements in chemistry, dissolution and *in vivo*Bioequivalence - None.

Filing Documentation- Annual report.

Level II Changes -

Classification–Same continuous campus, Common personnel, No other changes. Test Documentation–

- Application/ compendial requirements
- Notification of Location of newsite
- Updated batch records
- SUPAC – MR - Multi-point dissolution profiles(15,30,45,60 and 120 min)USP buffer media at pH 4.5-7.5 forextended release). Three differentMedia (e.g., Water, 0.1N HCl, andUSP buffer media at pH 4.5 and 6.8for delayed release)until 80% ofDrug Released.

Filing Documentation- Annual report.

Level III Changes -

Classification– Different campus, Different personnel. Test Documentation–

- Application/compendial requirements.
- Notification of Location of new site.
- Updated batch record.
- SUPAC - IR: Multi-point dissolution profile in the application/ compendial medium.
- SUPAC - MR: Multi-point dissolution profiles (15, 30, 45, 60 and 120 min) USP buffer media at pH 4.5-7.5 for extended release). Three different Media (e.g., Water, 0.1N HCl, and USP buffer media at pH 4.5

and 6.8 for delayed release) until 80 % of Drug Released.

Filing Documentation- Annual report prior approval of supplement.

C. Changes in Batch Size (Scale-Up/Scale-Down):

- Post-approval changes in the size of a batch from the pivotal/pilot scale bio batch material to larger or smaller production batches call for submission of additional information in the application.
- Scale-down below 100,000 dosage units is not covered by this guidance.

Level I Changes -

Classification- Change in batch size, up to and including a factor of 10 times the size of the pilot/biobatch.

Test Documentation– Updated batch records application/compendial requirements stability. Filing Documentation- Annual report (long term stability data).

Level II Changes -

Classification- Changes in batch size beyond a factor of ten times the size of the pilot or biobatch, No other changes.

Test Documentation–

- Chemistry Documentation Application/ compendial release requirements. Notification of change and submission of updated batch records. Stability testing: One batch with three months accelerated stability data and one batch on long-term stability.
- Dissolution Documentation-Case B testing.
- *In Vivo* Bioequivalence - None.

Filing Documentation- Changes being effected supplement; annual report (long-term stability data).

D. Manufacturing Changes:

Manufacturing changes may affect both equipment used in the manufacturing process and the process itself.

i)Equipment -

Level I Changes:

Classification- Alternate equipment of the same design and principles as automated equipment. Test Documentation– Updated batch records, Application/compendial requirements and stability. Filing Documentation- Prior approval supplement with justification for change; annual report (long-term stability data).

Level II Changes:

Classification- Change to equipment of different design and principle.

Test Documentation– Updated batch records, Application/compendial requirements and stability.

- SUPAC – IR - Multi-point dissolution profiles in multiple media.
- SUPAC – MR - Multi-point dissolution profiles in multiple media. Filing Documentation- Annual report and changes being Effected Supplement.

ii)Process -

Level I Changes:

Classification- Alternate equipment of the same design and principles as automated equipment. Test Documentation– Updated batch records, Application/compendial requirements and stability. Filing Documentation- Annual report.

Level II Changes:

Classification- This category includes process changes including changes such as mixing times and operating speeds outside of application/ validation ranges.

Test Documentation– Updated batch records, Application/compendial requirements and stability.

- SUPAC - IR - Multi-point dissolution profile.
- SUPAC- MR - Multi-point dissolution profiles in multiple media.
- SUPAC – SS - *In vitro* release test Documentation.

Filing Documentation- Changes being effected supplement; annual report (long term stability data).

Level III Changes:

Classification- Changes in the type of process used (e.g. wet granulation to direct compression). Test Documentation– Updated batch records, Application/compendial requirements, stability, bio-study and IVIVC.

- SUPAC - IR - Multi-point dissolution profile.
- SUPAC- MR - Multi-point dissolution profiles in multiple media.

Filing Documentation- Prior approval supplement with justification; annual report (long-term stability data).

INTRODUCTION TO PLATFORM TECHNOLOGY:

Platform technologies: Platform technologies are systems that distribute the system out into different levels of abstraction. This is done in order to differentiate between core – platform – functions, and the application layer that sits on top of, and draws upon, these underlying common services.

Pharmaceutical Platform technologies:

- Pharmaceutical Platform technologies are considered a valuable tool to improve efficiency and quality in drug product development. The basic idea is that a platform, in combination with a risk-based approach, is the most systematic method to leverage prior knowledge for a given new molecule.Platform technology is becoming a popular industry approach for bioprocessing.

Importance platform technology:

- Platform companies move faster than their traditional counterparts. When your core products and services frequently change, it forces your employees and your organization to embrace change quickly.

Types of platform technology:

- Operating systems provide the basic services required to use hardware.Computing Platforms.

  - Database Platforms.
  - Storage Platforms.
  - Application Platforms.
  - Mobile Platforms.
  - Web Platforms.

CHAPTER II

TECHNOLOGY TRANSFER

What is technology transfer?

- Transfer of technology is defined as a "logical procedure that controls the transfer of any process together with its documentation and professional expertise between developments or between manufacture sites."
- Technology transfer is both integral and critical to the drug discovery and development process for new medical products.
- Technology transfer is helpful to develop dosage forms in various ways as it provides efficiency in process, maintains quality of product, helps to achieve standardized process which facilitates cost effective production. It is the process by which by an original innovator of technology makes it technology available to commercial partner that will exploit the technology.
- In pharmaceutical industry, "Technology transfer "refers to the processes of successful progress from drug discovery to product development, clinical trials and ultimately full scale commercialization.
- Technology transfer is important for such researcher to materialize on a larger scale for commercialization especially in the case of developing product. Technology transfer includes not only patentable aspects of production but also includes the business processes such as knowledge and skills.

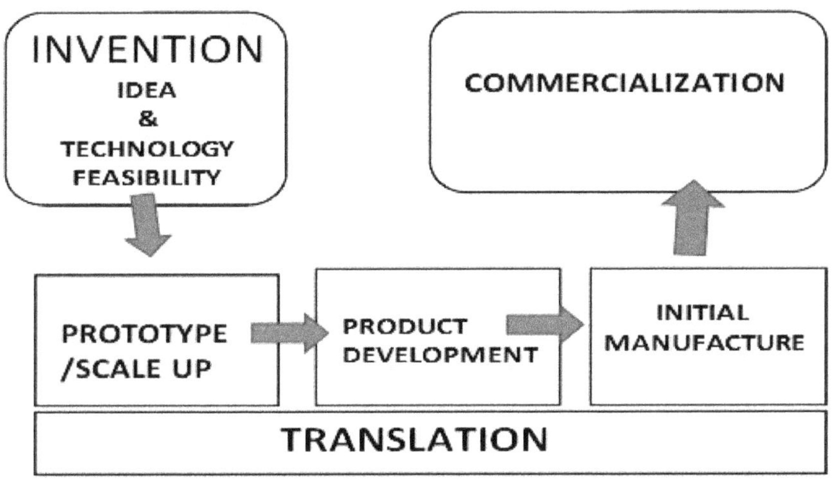

Fig 2.1: Different stages of technology transfer

Facts of technology transfer

The transfer of technology could happen in following ways

- Government labs to private sector firms.
- Between private sector firms of same country.
- Between private sector firms of different country.
- From academia to private sector firms.

WHO guidelines for Technology Transfer (TT)

These guiding principles on transfer of technology are intended to serve as a framework which can be applied in a flexible manner rather than as strict rigid guidance. Focus has been placed on the quality aspects, in line with WHO's mandate.

1. Transfer of processes to an alternative site occurs at some stage in the life-cycle of most products, from development, scale-up, manufacturing, production and launch, to the post- approval phase.
2. Transfer of technology is defined as "a logical procedure that controls the transfer of any process together with its documentation and professional expertise between development and manufacture or between manufacture sites". It is a systematic procedure that is followed in order to pass the documented knowledge and experience gained during development and or commercialization to an appropriate, responsible and authorized party.
3. Literature searches revealed little information on the subject originating from national or regional regulatory bodies. Guidance on intra-company transfers was prepared by the International Society for Pharmaceutical Engineering (ISPE).
4. The ever changing business strategies of pharmaceutical companies increasingly involve intra- and intercompany transfers of technology for reasons such as the need for additional capacity, relocation of operations or consolidations and mergers. The WHO Expert Committee on Specifications for Pharmaceutical Preparations, therefore, recommended in its 42nd report that WHO address this issue through preparation of WHO guidelines on this matter.
5. Transfer of technology requires a documented, planned approach using trained and knowledgeable personnel working within a quality system, with documentation of data covering all aspects of development, production and quality control. Usually there is a sending unit (SU), a receiving unit (RU) and the unit managing the process, which may or may not be a separate entity.

6. For successful transfer, the following **general principles** and requirements should be met:

    - The project plan should encompass the quality aspects of the project and be based upon the principles of quality risk management (QRM).
    - The capabilities of the SU and the RU should be similar, but not necessarily identical, and facilities and equipment should operate according to similar operating principles.
    - A comprehensive technical gap analysis between the SU and RU including technical risk assessment and potential regulatory gaps,

should be performed as needed.

- Adequately trained staff should be available or should be trained at the RU: Regulatory requirements in the countries of the SU and the RU, and in any countries where the product is intended to be supplied, should be taken into account and interpreted consistently throughout any transfer programme project and there should be effective process and product knowledge transfer.

7. Technology transfer can be considered successful if there is documented evidence that the RU can routinely reproduce the transferred product, process or method against a predefined set of specifications as agreed with the SU.
8. In the event that the RU identifies particular problems with the process during the transfer, the RU should communicate them back to the SU to ensure continuing knowledge management.
9. Technology transfer projects, particularly those between different companies, have legal and economic implications. If such issues, which may include intellectual property rights, royalties, pricing, conflict of interest and confidentiality, are expected to impact on open communication of technical matters in any way, they should be addressed before and during planning and execution of the transfer. Any lack of transparency may lead to ineffective transfer of technology.
10. Some of the responsibilities outlined in this document for the SU may also be considered to be part of the management unit responsibilities. The guidelines address the following areas:

- Transfer of development and production (processing, packaging and cleaning).
- Transfer of analytical methods for quality assurance and quality control.
- Skills assessment and training.
- Organization and management of the transfer.
- Assessment of premises and equipment.
- Documentation; and qualification and validation.

Terminologies used in technology Transfer

Acceptance criteria Measurable terms under which test results will be considered acceptable. ***Bracketing*** An experimental design to test only the extremes of, for example, dosage strength. The design assumes that the extremes will be representative of all the samples between the extremes.

Change control (C/C) A formal system by which qualified representatives of appropriate disciplines review proposed or actual changes that might affect a validated status. The intent is to determine the need for action that would ensure that the system is maintained in a validated state. ***Commissioning*** The setting up, adjustment and testing of equipment or a system to ensure that it meets all the requirements, as specified in the user requirement specification, and capacities as specified by the designer or developer. Commissioning is carried out before qualification and validation.

Corrective action (C/A) Any action to be taken when the results of monitoring at a critical control point indicate a loss of control.

Critical Having the potential to impact product quality or performance in a significant way. ***Critical control point (CCP)*** A step at which control can be applied and is essential to prevent or eliminate a pharmaceutical quality hazard or reduce it to an acceptable level.

Design qualification (DQ) Documented evidence that the premises, supporting systems, utilities, equipment and processes have been designed in accordance with the requirements of good manufacturing practices (GMP).

Design space The multidimensional combination and interaction of input variables (e.g. material attributes) and process parameters that have been demonstrated to provide assurance of quality.

Drug master file (DMF) Detailed information concerning a specific facility, process or product submitted to the drug regulatory authority, intended for the incorporation into the application for marketing authorization.

Gap analysis Identification of critical elements of a process which are available at the SU but are missing from the RU.

Good Manufacturing Practices (GMP) That part of quality assurance which ensures that products are consistently produced and controlled to the quality standards appropriate to their intended use and as required by the marketing authorization.

Inter-company transfer A transfer of technology between sites of different companies.

Intra-company transfer A transfer of technology between sites of the same group of companies. ***In-process control (IPC)*** Checks performed during production in order to monitor and, if necessary, to adjust the process to ensure that the product conforms to its specifications. The control of the environment or equipment may also be regarded as a part of in-process control.

Installation qualification (IQ) The performance of tests to ensure that the installations (such as machines, measuring devices, utilities and manufacturing areas) used in a manufacturing process are appropriately selected and correctly installed and operate in accordance with established specifications.

Operational qualification (OQ) Documented verification that the system or subsystem performs as intended over all anticipated operating ranges.

Performance qualification (PQ) Documented verification that the equipment or system operates consistently and gives reproducibility within defined specifications and parameters for prolonged periods.

Process validation Documented evidence which provides a high degree of assurance that a specific process will consistently result in a product that meets its predetermined specifications and quality characteristics.

Quality assurance (QA) Quality assurance is a wide-ranging concept covering all matters that individually or collectively influence the quality of a product. The totality of the arrangements made with the objective of ensuring that pharmaceutical products are of the quality required for their intended use.

Quality control (QC) Quality control covers all measures taken, including the setting of specifications, sampling, testing and analytical clearance, to ensure that starting materials, intermediates, packaging materials and finished pharmaceutical products conform with established specifications for identity, strength, purity and other characteristics.

Qualification Action of proving and documenting that any premises, systems and equipment are properly installed, and/or work correctly and lead to the expected results. Qualification is often a part (the initial stage) of validation, but the individual qualification steps alone do not constitute process validation.

Quality risk management (QRM) Quality risk management is a systematic process for the assessment, control, communication and review of risks to the quality of the pharmaceutical product across the product lifecycle.

Receiving unit (RU) The involved disciplines at an organization where a designated product, process or method is expected to be transferred.

Sending unit (SU) The involved disciplines at an organization where a designated product, process or method is expected to be transferred from.

Spiking The addition of a known amount of a compound to a standard, sample or placebo, typically for the purpose of confirming the performance of an analytical procedure.

Standard operating procedure (SOP) An authorized written procedure giving instructions for performing operations not necessarily specific to a given product or material (e.g. equipment operation, maintenance and cleaning; validation; cleaning of premises and environmental control; sampling and inspection).

Transfer of technology (TOT) A logical procedure that controls the transfer of an established process together with its documentation and professional expertise to site capable of reproducing the process and its support functions to a predetermined level of performance.

Validation Action of proving and documenting that any process, procedure or method actually and consistently leads to the expected results.

Validation master plan (VMP) A high-level document that establishes an umbrella validation plan for the entire project and summarizes the manufacturer's overall philosophy and approach, to be used for establishing performance adequacy. It provides information on the manufacturer's validation work programme and defines details of and timescales for the validation work to be performed, including a statement of the responsibilities of those implementing the plan.

Validation protocol (or plan) (VP) A document describing the activities to be performed in a validation, including the acceptance criteria for the approval of a manufacturing process – or a part thereof – for routine use.

Validation report (VR) A document in which the records, results and evaluation of a completed validation programme are assembled and summarized. It may also contain proposals for the improvement of processes and/or equipment.

Technology Transfer Protocol

The transfer protocol should list the intended sequential stages of the transfer. The protocol should include:

- objective;
- scope;
- key personnel and their responsibilities;
- a parallel comparison of materials, methods and equipment;
- the transfer stages with documented evidence that each critical stage has been satisfactorily accomplished before the next commences;
- identification of critical control points;
- experimental design and acceptance criteria for analytical methods;
- information on trial production batches, qualification batches and process validation;
- change control for any process deviations encountered;
- assessment of end-product;
- arrangements for keeping retention samples of active ingredients, intermediates and finished products, and information on reference substances where applicable; and
- Conclusion, including signed-off approval by project manager.

Quality risk management

Two primary principles of quality risk management are:

- The evaluation of the risk to quality should be based on scientific knowledge and ultimately link to the protection of the patient; and
- The level of effort, formality and documentation of the quality risk management process should be commensurate with the level of risk.

Quality risk management is a systematic process for the assessment, control, communication and review of risks to the quality of the drug (medicinal) product across the product lifecycle. A model for quality risk management is outlined in the Figure 2.

Responsibilities

Quality risk management activities are usually, but not always, undertaken by interdisciplinary teams. When teams are formed, they should include experts from the appropriate areas (e.g., quality unit, business development, engineering, regulatory affairs, production operations, sales and marketing, legal, statistics and clinical) in addition to individuals who are knowledgeable about the quality risk management process.

Initiating a Quality Risk Management Process

Quality risk management should include systematic processes designed to coordinate, facilitate and improve science-based decision making with respect to risk. Possible steps used to initiate and plan a quality risk management process might include the following :

- Define the problem and/or risk question, including pertinent assumptions identifying the potential for risk;
- Assemble background information and/ or data on the potential hazard, harm or human health impact relevant to the risk assessment;
- Identify a leader and necessary resources;
- Specify a timeline, deliverables and appropriate level of decision making for the risk management process.

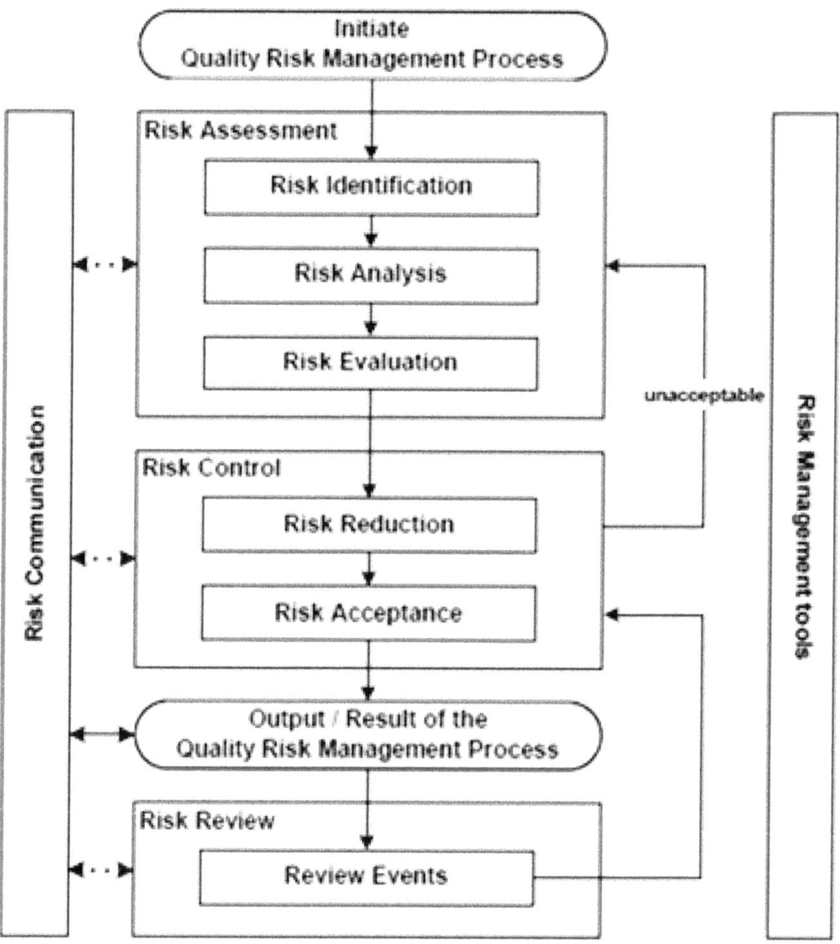

Fig 2.2: Overview of a typical Quality risk management process

Risk Assessment

Risk assessment consists of the identification of hazards and the analysis and evaluation of risks associated with exposure to those hazards. Quality risk assessments begin with a well-defined problem description or risk question. Three fundamental questions are often helpful:

- What might go wrong?

- What is the likelihood (probability) it will go wrong?
- What are the consequences (severity)?
- *Risk Identification*

It is a systematic use of information to identify hazards referring to the risk question or problem description. Information can include historical data, theoretical analysis, informed opinions, and the concerns of stakeholders. Risk identification addresses the "What might go wrong?" question, including identifying the possible consequences

Risk analysis

Risk analysis is the estimation of the risk associated with the identified hazards. It is the qualitative or quantitative process of linking the likelihood of occurrence and severity of harms. ***Risk Evaluation***

It compares the identified and analyzed risk against given risk criteria. The output of a risk assessment is either a quantitative estimate of risk or a qualitative description of a range of risk. When risk is expressed quantitatively, a numerical probability is used. Alternatively, risk can be expressed using qualitative descriptors, such as "high", "medium", or "low", which should be defined in as much detail as possible.

Risk Control Risk control includes decision making to reduce and/or accept risks. The purpose of risk control is to reduce the risk to an acceptable level. Risk control might focus on the following questions:

- Is the risk above an acceptable level?
- What can be done to reduce or eliminate risks?
- What is the appropriate balance among benefits, risks and resources?
- Are new risks introduced as a result of the identified risks being controlled?

Risk Reduction

Risk reduction focuses on processes for mitigation or avoidance of quality risk when it exceeds a specified (acceptable) level. Risk reduction might include actions taken to mitigate the severity and probability of harm. Processes that improve the detectability of hazards and quality risks might also be used as part of a risk control strategy.

Risk communication

Risk communication is the sharing of information about risk and risk management between the decision makers and others. Parties can communicate at any stage of the risk management process. The output/ result of the quality risk management process should be appropriately communicated and documented.

Risk review

A mechanism to review or monitor events should be implemented. The output/results of the risk management process should be reviewed to take into account new knowledge and experience. The frequency of any review should be based upon the level of risk. Risk review might include reconsideration of risk acceptance decisions.

Risk management methodology

Quality risk management supports a scientific and practical approach to decision-making. It provides documented, transparent and reproducible methods to accomplish steps of the quality risk management process based on current knowledge about assessing the probability, severity and sometimes detectability of the risk. The pharmaceutical industry and regulators can access and manage risk using recognized risk management tools and/or internal procedures (e.g., standard operating procedures). Below is a non-exhaustive list of some of these tools.

- Basic risk management facilitation methods (flowcharts, check sheets etc.);
- Failure Mode Effects Analysis (FMEA);
- Failure Mode, Effects and Criticality Analysis (FMECA);
- Fault Tree Analysis (FTA);
- Hazard Analysis and Critical Control Points (HACCP);
- Hazard Operability Analysis (HAZOP);
- Preliminary Hazard Analysis (PHA);
- Risk ranking and filtering;

- Supporting statistical tools.

Transfer from R & D to production (Process, packaging and cleaning)

- It should be established at the outset whether the intention is to perform single-batch manufacture, continuous production or campaigns, and whether the RU can accommodate the intended production capacity.
- Consideration should be given to the level and depth of detail to be transferred to support production and any further development or process optimization at the RU as intended under the transfer project plan.
- The SU and the RU should jointly develop a protocol for the transfer of relevant information related to the manufacturing process under consideration from the SU to the RU, as well as the development of an equivalent process at the RU.

Process

The SU should provide a detailed characterization of the product, including its qualitative and quantitative composition, physical description, method of manufacture, in-process controls and specifications, packaging components and configurations, and any special safety and handling considerations. The SU should provide any information on the history of process development which may be required to enable the RU to perform any further development and/or process optimization intended after successful transfer. Such information may include the following:

- ***information on clinical development***, e.g. information on the rationale for the synthesis, route and form selection, technology selection, equipment, clinical tests, and product composition;
- ***information on scale-up activities***: process optimization, statistical optimization of critical process parameters, pilot report and/or information on pilot-scale development activities indicating the number and disposition of batches manufactured; and

- ***information or report on full-scale development activities***, indicating the number and disposition of batches manufactured, and deviation and change control reports which led to the current manufacturing.

The SU should provide to the RU information on any health, safety and environmental issues associated with the manufacturing processes to be transferred, and resulting implications, e.g. need for gowning or protective clothing.

The SU should provide to the RU information on current processing and testing, including but not limited to:

- a detailed description of facility requirements and equipment ;
- process technology selection;
- information on starting materials, applicable MSDs and storage requirements for raw materials and finished products;
- description of manufacturing steps (narrative and process maps or flow charts), including qualification of in-processing hold times and conditions, order and method of raw material addition and bulk transfers between processing steps;
- description of analytical methods;
- in-process controls, including, e.g. identification of critical performance aspects for specific dosage forms, identification of process control points, product quality attributes and qualification of critical processing parameter ranges, statistical process control (SPC) charts;
- validation information, e.g. validation plans and reports, and annual product reviews;
- stability information; and an authorized set of SOPs and work instructions for manufacturing.

Packaging

It should follow the same procedural patterns as those of the production transfer.

- ***Information on packaging*** to be transferred from the SU to the RU include specifications for a suitable container/closure system, as well as any relevant additional information on design, packing, processing or labeling requirements needed for qualification of packaging components at the RU.

- ***For quality control testing*** of packaging components, specifications should be provided for drawings, artwork, and material (glass, card, fibre board, etc.).

Based on the information provided, the RU should perform a suitability study for initial qualification of the packaging components. Packaging is considered suitable if it provides adequate protection (preventing degradation of the drug due to environmental influences), safety (absence of undesirable substances released into the product), compatibility (absence of interaction possibly affecting drug quality) and performance (functionality in terms of drug delivery).

Cleaning

During the manufacturing process, pharmaceutical products and APIs can be contaminated by other pharmaceutical products or APIs if processing different products. To minimize the risk of contamination and cross-contamination, operator exposure and environmental effects, adequate cleaning procedures are essential.

The SU should provide information on cleaning procedures in use at the SU to minimize cross- contamination due to residues from previous manufacturing steps, operator exposure and environmental impact, including: solubility information of active ingredients, excipients and vehicles.

Granularity of TT Process (API, excipients, finished products, packaging materials)

Starting materials

The specifications of the starting materials (APIs and excipients) to be used at the RU should be consistent with reference batches (development batches, biobatches or batches manufactured at the SU). Any properties which are likely to influence the process or product should be identified and characterized.

Active Pharmaceutical Ingredients (API)

The SU should provide the drug master file (DMF) and any relevant additional information on the API to the RU to be checked against the specifications of the API. The following information should be provided:

- manufacturer;
- flow chart of synthetic pathway, outlining the process, including entry points for raw materials, critical steps, process controls and intermediates;
- definitive form of the API (including photomicrographs and other relevant data) and any polymorphic and solvate forms;
- solubility profile;
- partition coefficient (including the method of determination);
- intrinsic dissolution rate (including the method of determination);
- particle size and distribution (including the method of determination);
- bulk physical properties, including data on bulk and tap density, surface area and porosity as appropriate;
- water content and determination of hygroscopicity, including water activity data and special handling requirements;
- microbiological considerations (including sterility, bacterial endotoxins and bioburden levels where the API supports microbiological growth) in accordance with regional pharmacopoeial requirements;
- specifications and justification for release and end-of-life limits;
- summary of stability studies conducted in conformity with current guidelines, including conclusions and recommendations on retest date;
- listing of potential and observed synthetic impurities, with data to support proposed specifications and typically observed levels;
- information on degradants, with a listing of potential and observed degradation products and data to support proposed specifications and typically observed levels;
- potency factor, indicating observed purity and justification for any recommended adjustment to the input quantity of API for product manufacturing, providing example calculations; and
- special considerations with implications for storage and/or handling, e.g. safety and environmental factors and sensitivity to heat, light or moisture.

Excipients

The excipients to be used have a potential impact on the final product. Their specifications as well as the DMF should, therefore, be made available by the SU for transfer to the RU site. The following information should be provided for all types of excipients:

- description of functionality, with justification for inclusion of any antioxidant, preservative or any excipient above recommended guidelines;
- manufacturer;
- specifications, i.e. monographs and additional information that may affect product processing or quality for compendia excipients, or a complete listing of specifications, including analytical methods and justification for release limits for non-compendial excipients. For excipients used for the first time in a human drug product or by a new route of administration, the same level of detail as for a drug substance should be provided;
- special considerations with implications for storage and/or handling, including but not limited to safety and environmental factors (e.g. as specified in material safety data sheets) and sensitivity to heat, light or moisture solubility; and
- regulatory considerations, i.e. compendial status and appropriate regulatory information for non-compendial excipients; information on residual solvents or organic volatile impurities; and documentation to support compliance with transmissible animal spongiform encephalopathy certification requirements (where applicable).

Finished Products Depending on the type of dosage form, the SU should provide relevant information on physical properties of excipients to the RU, including:

- definitive form (for solid and inhaled dosage forms);
- solubility profile (for solid, inhaled and transdermal dosage forms);
- partition coefficient, including the method of determination (for transdermal dosage forms);

- intrinsic dissolution rate, including the method of determination (for transdermal dosage forms);
- particle size and distribution, including the method of determination (for solid, inhaled and transdermal dosage forms);
- bulk physical properties, including data on bulk and tap density, surface area and porosity as appropriate (for solid and inhaled dosage forms);
- compaction properties (for solid dosage forms);
- melting point range (for semi-solid/topical dosage forms);
- pH range (for parenteral, semi-solid/topical, liquid and transdermal dosage forms);
- ionic strength (for parenteral dosage forms);
- specific density/gravity (for parenteral, semi-solid/topical, liquid and transdermal dosage forms);
- viscosity and/or viscoelasticity (for parenteral, semi-solid/topical, liquid and transdermal dosage forms);
- osmolarity (for parenteral dosage forms);
- water content and determination of hygroscopicity, including water activity data and special handling requirements (for solid and inhaled dosage forms);
- moisture content range (for parenteral, semi-solid/topical, liquid and transdermal dosage forms);
- microbiological considerations in accordance with regional pharmacopoeial requirements (for parenteral, semi-solid/topical, liquid, inhaled and transdermal dosage forms); and
- information on adhesives supporting compliance with peel, sheer and adhesion design criteria (for transdermal dosage forms).

Packaging

Information on packaging to be transferred from the SU to the RU include specifications for a suitable container/closure system, as well as any relevant additional information on design, packing, processing or labeling requirements needed for qualification of packaging components at the RU. For quality control testing of packaging components, specifications should be provided for drawings, artwork, material.

Documentation: The documents used in technology transfer are presented in table below.

Key task	Documentation provided by SU	Transfer documentation
Project definition	Project plan and quality plan (where separate documents), protocol, risk assessments, gap analysis	Project implementation plan **TOT protocol**
Quality agreement Facility assessment	Plans and layout of facility, buildings (construction, finish) Qualification status (DQ, IQ, OQ) and reports	Side-by-side comparison with RU facility and buildings; gap Analysis **Qualification protocol and report**
Health & Safety assessment	Product-specific waste management plans Contingency plans	
Skill set analysis and training	SOPs and training documentation (product-specific operations, analysis, testing)	Training protocols, assessment results
Analytical method transfer	Analytical method specifications and validation, including in-process quality control	Analytical methods transfer protocol and report
Starting material Evaluation Equipment selection and transfer	Specifications and additional information on APIs, excipients Inventory list of all equipment and systems, including makes, models, qualification status (IQ, OQ, PQ). Drawings, manuals, logs, SOPs (e.g. set-up, operation, cleaning, maintenance, calibration, storage)	Side-by-side comparison with RU equipment (makes, models, qualification status) Gap analysis. **Qualification and validation protocol and report**
Process transfer: manufacturing and packaging	Reference batches (clinical, dossier, bio-batches) Development report (manufacturing process rationale).History of critical analytical data Rationale for specifications, Change control documentation, Critical manufacturing process Parameters Process validation reports Drug master file. API validation status and report(s) Product stability data Current master batch manufacturing and packaging records List of all batches produced Deviation reports, Investigations, complaints, recalls Annual product review	History of process development at RU, Experiences at RU should be recorded for future reference Provisional batch mfg document (RU to develop) Provisional batch packaging document (RU to develop) Description of process at RU (narrative, process map, fl ow chart) **Process validation protocol and report**
Cleaning	Cleaning validation, Solubility information; therapeutic doses; category (toxicology); existing cleaning SOPs; validation reports chemical and micro; agents used; recovery study	Product- and site-specifi c cleaning SOPs at RU **Cleaning validation protocol and report**

Table 1. Documentation for transfer of technology (TOT)

Premises and Equipment

Premises

- The SU should provide information to the RU on the layout, construction and finish of all buildings and services (heating, ventilation and air-conditioning (HVAC), temperature, relative humidity, water, power, compressed air) impacting the product, process or method to be transferred.
- The SU should provide information on relevant health, safety and environmental issues, including:
- inherent risks of the manufacturing processes (e.g. reactive chemical hazards, exposure limits, fire and explosion risks).
- health and safety requirements to minimize operator exposure (e.g. atmospheric containment of pharmaceutical dust).
- Differences in building, construction layout and services between the SU and the RU should be listed and compared in view of the following considerations:
- buildings and services at the RU should be capable of accommodating the product, process or method under transfer to the agreed quality standard and production volume in compliance with GMP;

DQ, design qualification; IQ, installation qualification; OQ, operational qualification; API, active pharmaceutical ingredient; SOPs, standard operating procedures; RU, receiving unit.

- quality control laboratories should be equipped and capable of testing all APIs, excipients, intermediate and finished products, packaging components and cleaning validation samples;
- buildings intended for production of a highly sensitizing nature (e.g. penicillins and cytotoxic materials) should be dedicated for this purpose and located in a different facility from other production units; and
- health, safety and environmental issues, including waste management, emergency planning, minimization of operator exposure and environmental impact, should be addressed at the RU in compliance with any regulatory or company-developed rules, regulations and limits.

Equipment

The SU should provide a list of equipment, makes and models involved in the manufacture, filling, packing and/or control of the product, process or method to be transferred, together with existing qualification and validation documentation. Relevant documentation may include:

- drawings;
- manuals;
- maintenance logs;
- calibration logs; and
- SOPs (e.g. equipment set up, operation, cleaning, maintenance, calibration, storage).

The RU should review the information provided by the SU together with its own inventory list including the qualification status (IQ, OQ, PQ) of all equipment and systems, and perform a side- by-side comparison of equipment at the two sites in terms of their functionality, makes, models and qualification status.

Based on the side-by-side comparison, the RU should perform a gap analysis to identify requirements for adaptation of existing equipment, or acquisition of new equipment, to enable the RU to reproduce the process being transferred. GMP requirements should be satisfied, and intended production volumes and batch sizes (e.g. same, scaled-up or campaign) should be considered. Factors to be compared include:

- minimum and maximum capacity;
- material of construction;
- critical operating parameters;
- critical equipment components (e.g. filters, screens, temperature/ pressure sensors); and
- range of intended use.

The facility- and building-specific location of all equipment at the RU should be considered at the time of drawing up process maps or flow charts of the manufacturing process to be transferred, including movement of personnel and material.

The impact of manufacturing new products on products currently manufactured with the same equipment should be determined.

Where existing producing equipment needs to be adapted to be capable of reproducing the process being transferred, a detailed development project should be included in the transfer protocol.

New equipment should be designed and constructed to facilitate the process and ease cleaning and maintenance operations. Any newly acquired equipment should undergo a qualification protocol up to and including OQ level.

Applicable operating procedures for set-up, operation, cleaning, storage and maintenance should be developed by the conclusion of OQ. Supporting documents such as drawings of equipment and piping installations, manuals, maintenance logs and calibration logs should be retained.

Qualification and Validation General

- Qualification and validation of facilities, equipment, systems and procedures are essential to demonstrate that all critical stages of the transfer project have been completed successfully, enabling the RU to reproduce the product, process or method routinely to the specifications agreed with the SU.
- Validation performed as part of the transfer project should be documented in a validation master plan (VMP). The VMP should identify the stages which need to be validated and define acceptance criteria.
- For intra-company transfers, the RU should operate under the same VMP as the SU. For inter- company transfers, a VMP should be in place at the RU before the transfer.
- The RU should prepare a validation protocol (VP) for each sequential step. Successful execution of each VP should be documented in a validation report (VR).
- Setting up and commissioning of systems at the RU need to be completed before qualification and validation can be performed at the RU. The steps required for this purpose have been described in this guideline for buildings, services and equipment, manufacturing, packaging and cleaning and analytical testing. In brief, the following basic steps apply equally to each of these areas:
- the SU should provide information on materials, systems and procedures involved in the manufacturing of the product, process or method to be

transferred;

- the RU should review the information provided by the SU, and audit its current systems, equipment and processes, including non-process related practices and support services that impact the process;
- based on this review, the RU should either accept the information provided or develop it further to prepare site-specific procedures, SOPs, training programmes and protocols which will form the basis of the qualification and validation; and
- relevant staff, e.g. operators and analysts, should be trained in any new processes as required.
- Once the required systems and procedures have been commissioned at the RU, and successful training has been documented, qualification and validation of facility and equipment should be executed, followed by validation of analytical test methods, process validation for manufacturing and packaging, and cleaning validation.

    - The RU should review the gap analysis and prepare, where appropriate, VPs for the facility, services and equipment.
    - Both new and existing equipment should satisfy the VPs associated with purchase and design specifications, factory acceptance tests (FAT) if possible, IQ and OQ.
    - Performance qualification, including a further assessment of operating parameters with relation to product characteristics, should be established on commencement of trial batches.
    - Successful completion of qualification and validation should be documented in a report.

Quality Control:

Transfer of analytical methods should accommodate all the analytical testing required to demonstrate compliance of the product to be transferred with the registered specification.

Transfer of analytical methods used to test pharmaceutical products, their ingredients and cleaning (residue) samples, needs to be in place before process validation studies of manufacturing operations can be carried out.

The SU should prepare a protocol defining the steps to be undertaken for analytical method transfer. The analytical methods transfer protocol should describe the objective; scope; responsibilities of the SU and the RU; materials, methods and equipment; the experimental design and acceptance criteria; documentation (including information to be supplied with the results, and report forms to be used if any); deviations; references; signed approval; and details of reference samples (APIs, intermediates and finished products).

The SU's responsibilities for the transfer of analytical methods are to:

- provide method-specific training for analysts and other quality control staff;
- provide acceptance criteria and validation protocols for any RU training exercises;

- assist in analysis of quality control testing results;
- define and justify all methods to be transferred for testing a given product, ingredient or cleaning sample;
- define experimental design, sampling methods and acceptance criteria;
- provide any validation reports for methods under transfer, and demonstrate their robustness;
- provide data for the equipment used and any standard reference samples; and
- provide approved SOPs used in testing. The RU's responsibilities are to:
- review analytical methods provided by the SU, and formally agree on acceptance criteria before execution of the transfer protocol;
- ensure that the necessary equipment for quality control is available and qualified at the RU site. Equipment should be replicated where possible, but it is accepted that different models, e.g. spectrometers and chromatographs, could already be in place;

- ensure that adequately trained and experienced personnel is in place for analytical testing;
- provide a documentation system capable of recording receipt and testing of samples. A suggested analytical training protocol would be as follows:

    - SU and RU analysts assay two retained samples from SU;
    - SU and RU analysts then assay two sub-potent samples (available from SU or spiked);
    - SU and RU analysts assay samples taken from RU production;

- RU analyst provides sufficient replicate analyses to enable a significance test (e.g. student's against the established method at the SU site; and
    - a similar exercise should be undertaken for analysis of low levels of APIs.
    - All training activities and outcomes should be documented.

Analytical methods Transfer

The analytical methods transfer protocol should cover the following sections:

- objective;
- scope;
- responsibilities of the SU and the RU;
- materials, methods and equipment;
- the experimental design and acceptance criteria;
- documentation (including information to be supplied with the results, and report forms to be used if any);
- deviations;
- references;
- signed approval; and
- details of reference samples (APIs, intermediates and finished products). Successful transfer and validation of analytical methods should be documented in a report.

Approved regulatory bodies and agencies

The principal regulatory bodies entrusted with the responsibility of ensuring the approval, production and marketing of quality drugs in India at reasonable prices are:

- ***The Central Drug Standards and Control Organization (CDSCO),*** located under the aegis of the Ministry of Health and Family Welfare. The CDSCO prescribes standards and measures for ensuring the safety, efficacy and quality of drugs, cosmetics, diagnostics and devices in the country. Regulates the market authorization of new drugs and clinical trials standards; supervises drug imports and approves licences to manufacture the above-mentioned products.

- ***The Drugs Controller General of India (DCGI),*** With respect to licencing and quality control issues, market authorization is regulated by the Central Drug Controller, Ministry of Health and Family Welfare, Department of Biotechnology, Ministry of Science and Technology (DST) and Department of Environment, Ministry of Environment and Forests. State drug controllers have the authority to issue licences for the manufacture of approved drugs and monitor quality control, along with the ***Central Drug Standards Control Organization (CDSCO).***
- ***The Food and Drug Administration (FDA or USFDA)*** is a federal agency of the United States Department of Health and Human Services, one of the United States federal executive departments. The FDA is responsible for protecting and promoting public health through the Control and supervision of food safety, tobacco products, dietary supplements, prescriprion and over the counter pharmaceutical drugs (medications), vaccines, biopharmaceuticals, blood transfusions, medical, electromagnetic radiation emitting devices (ERED), cosmetics, animal foods & feed[4] and veterinary products.
- ***The Therapeutic Goods Administration (TGA)*** is part of the Australian Government Department of Health, and is responsible for regulating therapeutic goods including prescription medicines, vaccines, sunscreens, vitamins and minerals, medical devices, blood and blood products. Almost any product for which therapeutic claims are made must be entered in the Australian Register of Therapeutic Goods (ARTG) before it can be supplied in Australia.
- ***Medicines and Healthcare products Regulatory Agency (MHRA)*** regulates medicines, medical devices and blood components for transfusion in the UK.

Commercialization - practical aspects and problems (case studies)

Technology transfer are discussed with certain practical studies.

Case Study 1

The blending of drug with excipients is presented in table 2. [3] ***Factors considered in the proposed technology transfer (scale up)*** Geometric Similarity: Ratio of all lengths constant (constant fill ratio) Dynamic Similarity: Maintenance of Forces (Froude number).

Kinematic Similarity: Maintaining a consistent number or revolutions

Scale	Amount (kg)	Blender Capacity	Blending Speed (rpm)	Blending Time (min)	Nrev	Volume Fill Ratio (%)
Laboratory	2	8 qt	25	12	300	~50
Pilot	40	7.5 cu.ft	15	20	300	~50
Commercial	180	30 cu. Ft	10	30	300	~50

Table 2, Scale-up in QbD Approach: Blending

Case Study 2 (Drug layering on MCC spheres)

Equipment of production having greatest similitude (geometric) to the intended to commercial scale process, similar particle trajectories and dynamics enables maintenance of process parameters through scale-up with the exception of air-flow which is linearly scaled (Figure 3, Table 3).

Conclusion of case study 2

Air flow rate and total spray rate were adjusted to obtain uniform coating of drug on MCC spheres. Assay of the formulation was 99.9% in both pilot batch and commercial batch.

	Pilot batches	**Commercial scale**
Starting Batch Size	40 kg	140 kg
Ending Batch Size	56 kg	198 kg
Estimated use of capacity	50%-70%	56%-79%
Number of Partition(s)	1	3
Partition height	30-50 mm	30-50 mm
Nozzle	1.2 mm	1.2 mm
Product Temperature	44-48 C	44-48 C
Air Flow Rate	**810±90 cfm**	**2430±270 cfm**
Spray Rate per nozzle	135±25 g/min	135±25 g/min
Total Spray Rate	**135±25 g/min**	**405±75 g/min**
Atomization Pressure per nozzle	2.5-2.9 bar	2.5-2.9 bar

Table 3, Parameters for pilot and verification batches at commercial scale

TT agencies in India - APCTD, NRDC, TIFAC, BCIL, TBSE /SIDBI

Asian and Pacific Centre for Transfer of Technology (APCTT)

It is a United Nations Regional Institution under the Economic and Social Commission for Asia and the Pacific (ESCAP) established in 1977 in Bangalore, India. In 1993, the Centre moved to New Delhi, India. APCTT promotes transfer of technology to and from small- and medium-scale enterprises (SMEs) in Asia and the Pacific. APCTT implements development projects funded by international donors aimed at strengthening the environment for technology transfer among SMEs. The objective of APCTT is to strengthen the technology transfer capabilities in the region and to facilitate import/export of environmentally sound technologies to/from the member countries.

National Research Development Corporation (NRDC)

National Research Development Corporation (NRDC) was established in 1953 by the Government of India, with the primary objective to promote, develop and commercialise the technologies / know-how / inventions / patents / processes emanating from various national R&D institutions / Universities and is presently working under the administrative control of the Dept. of Scientific & Industrial Research, Ministry of Science & Technology. During the past six decade of its existence and in pursuance of its corporate goals, NRDC has forged strong links with the scientific and industrial community in India and abroad. It is recognized as a large repository of wide range of technologies spread over almost all areas of industries, viz. Agriculture and Agro-processing, Chemicals including Pesticides, Drugs and Pharmaceuticals, Bio Technology, Metallurgy, Electronics and Instrumentation, Building Materials, Mechanical, Electrical and Electronics etc. It has licensed the indigenous technology to more than 4800 entrepreneurs and helped to establish a large number of small and medium scale industries. NRDC also undertakes number of activities such as meritorious inventions awards, Techno- Commercial support, Technical and financial assistance for IPR Protection, Value addition services and support for further development of technologies and much more.

Technology information, Forecasting and assesemement Council (TIFAC)

TIFAC is an autonomous organization set up in 1988 under the Department of Science & Technology to look ahead in technology domain, assess the technology trajectories, and support innovation by networked actions in selected areas of national importance TIFAC embarked upon the major task of formulating a Technology Vision for the country in various emerging technology areas. Under the leadership of Dr. APJ Abdul Kalam, Technology Vision 2020 exercise led to set of 17 documents, including sixteen technology areas and one on services. In more than 25 years of its service to the nation, it has delivered number of technology assessment and foresight reports. While inaugurating the 103rd Indian Science Congress in Mysuru, Hon'ble Prime Minister of India Shri Narendra Modi released the Technology Vision 2035 prepared by TIFAC.This is being followed by release of Technology Roadmaps in 12 thematic areas of national priorities and importance • Education, Medical Science & Health Care, Food and Agriculture, Water, Energy, Environment, Habitat, Transportation, Infrastructure, Manufacturing, Materials and Information & Communication Technologies (ICT).

Biotech Consortium India Limited (BCIL)

Biotech Consortium India Limited (BCIL), New Delhi was incorporated as public limited company in 1990 under The Companies Act, 1956. The consortium is promoted by the Department of Biotechnology, Government of India and financed by the All India Financial Institutions and some corporate sectors BCIL 's major functions include the development and transfer of technology for the commercialisation of biotechnology products, project consultancy, biosafety awareness and human resource development BCIL has been successfully managing several Flagship schemes and Programmes of the Department of Biotechnology, Government of India. Most notable include Biotechnology Industry Partnership Programme, 2. Biotechnology Industrial Training Programme and Small Business Innovation Research Initiative

Technology Bureau for Small Enterprises (TBSE)/ Small Industries Development Bank of India (SIDBI).

The Technology Bureau for Small Enterprises (TBSE) is a platform for MSMEs to tap opportunities at the global level for the acquisition of technology or establishing business collaboration. TBSE is a result of the cooperative initiative of the United Nations' Asian and Pacific Centre for Transfer of Technology (APCTT) and Small Industries Development Bank of India (SIDBI) in 1995. TBSE also receives partial funding from the Office of DC (SSI), Government of India. Features of TBSE Offering a professionally managed system for the reasons of technology and collaboration exploration helping in the building up of confidence between potential partner. It providing an opportunity to global technology market through the process of networking. Taking up project appraisal and the preparation of a business plan. The new technologies for the reason of transfer are sourced from countries namely China, Philippines, South Korea, Australia, Germany, as well as the U.S.

TT related documentation - confidentiality agreement, licensing, MoUs, legal issues. [5] Confidentiality Agreements

The aim of a confidentiality agreement is to protect all information of party entering negotiations. Before any concrete negotiations on the transfer of a technology can really start all parties involved must be able to evaluate the technology offered. Both the technological and the commercial possibilities of the offer will thereby be taken into account. Before giving anybody access to your technology a confidentiality agreement should be drafted with discussion on the main topics to be addressed in such agreement keeping in mind that all the standard clauses of an agreement should also be included (parties, term and termination, applicable law). The first item in any confidentiality agreement should be a brief but clear description of the technology that will be transferred. What are the main specifications of this technology and what is its relevant application? In this same disposition of the agreement a reference to the property rights of the party offering can be made.

Licensing

The legal core of the transfer of technology is constituted by a licensing agreement. By signing this agreement the owner of a technology, the licenser, gives the right to another company, the licensee, to make use of this technology. A licence does not alter the property rights of the owner: he remains the only proprietor of the technology. He could also sell his technology whereby the buyer becomes the owner and replaces the seller. But if an owner of a technology prefers to enter into an agreement with a licensee he will give him limited rights. The licensee cannot dispose of the technology but he can use it. This use will be more or less limited. A limitation in time, in geographical market, in product market or in the application can be introduced in a licence. The licence will determine the relationship between the licenser and licensee for the whole duration of their co-operation and a lot of questions will have to be answered before this relationship can start.

Memoranda of Understanding (MOUs)

Often collaborative research efforts with outside institutions are defined in Memoranda of Understanding (MOU) before other agreements are executed. An MOU typically defines how intellectual property will be shared and the roles and responsibilities of the involved parties. If you are planning to enter into a collaborative relationship with an outside party, it is important to discuss the possibility of an MOU. Office of Technology Commercialization is responsible for drafting MOUs related to collaborative research. MOUs typically identify a lead institution for managing intellectual property and provide details on how licensing income will be shared.

Legal Issues

The following types legal issues are generally observed in technology transfer.

- Legal contractual agreements
- Tax implications
- Legal issues in intellectual property transaction
- Problems associated with IPR litigation
- Legislations covering IPRs in India.

CHAPTER III

REGULATORY AFFAIRS

Definition:

Regulatory Affairs (RA), also called Government Affairs, is a profession developed from the desire of governments to protect public health by controlling the safety and efficacy of products in areas including pharmaceuticals, veterinary medicines, medical devices, pesticides, agrochemicals, foods, cosmetics and complementary medicines etc.

As a discipline, regulatory affairs cover a broad range of specific skills and occupations. Under the best of circumstances, it is composed of a group of people who act as a liaison between the government, industry, and consumers to make sure that marketed products are safe and effective when used as it advertised.

People who work in regulatory affairs negotiate the interaction between the regulators (the government), the regulated (industry), and the market (consumers) to get good products to the market and to keep them there while preventing bad products from being sold.

Pharmaceutical Drug Regulatory Affairs (DRA) is a dynamic field that includes scientific, legal and commercial aspect of drug-development.

Drug development to commercialization is highly regulated. Every drug before getting market approval must undergo rigorous scrutiny and clinical trials to ensure its safety, efficacy and quality. These standards are set by regulatory authorities of their respective countries such as FDA in US and CDSCO in India etc.

Regulation of Drug products involve following areas –

- Non-clinical and Clinical Drug Development Guidelines
- Licensing (Patent)
- Drug Registration
- Manufacturing
- Quality and safety Guidance
- Pricing and Trademark
- Marketing, Import and Distribution of Drug products

- Pharmacovigilance (Adverse Drug Reactions monitoring)

Year	Event	Purpose
1906	Pure Food and Drug Act	Prevent false claims
1930	FDA takes its current name	Agency is purely regulatory – no research functions
1938	Federal Food, Drug, and Cosmetic Act	Require proof of safety before marketing
1949	First publication of FDA "Guidance to Industry"	Address the appraisal of toxic chemicals in foods
1962	Kefauver–Harris Drug Amendments	Require proof of efficacy and safety before marketing
1987	Prescription Drug Marketing Act	Ensure that pharmaceutical products purchased by consumers are safe and effective, and free from counterfeit, adulterated, misbranded, subpotent, or expired drugs
2004	Pharmaceutical cGMPs for the 21st Century – A Risk-Based Approach	Emphasize risk-based approaches to development and manufacturing
2004	PAT – A Framework for Innovative Pharmaceutical Development, Manufacturing, and Quality Assurance	Achieve greater understanding of drug development and manufacturing processes. Data acquisition and multivariate analysis cited as important tools
2005	ICH Harmonized Tripartite Guideline: Pharmaceutical Development, Q8	Foster quality by design and the understanding of design space – emphasis on design of experiments to define interactions and work in multidimensions
2005	ICH Harmonized Tripartite Guideline: Quality Risk Management, Q9	Encourage the use of quality risk-management tools in all phases of a product's lifecycle
2007	ICH Harmonized Tripartite Guideline: Pharmaceutical Quality System, Q10	Enhance science- and risk-based regulatory approaches

Table 1 - Historical Overview of RA (Key regulatory events with year)

Regulatory Authorities -

Public health being the prime concern, it is necessary that the drug/drug product available for human/veterinary use and medical devices must not only be effective but also be safe for the intended use. To ensure this, various territorial regulatory bodies came into existence.

Major regulatory agencies include World Health Organization (WHO), United States Food and Drug Administration (USFDA, United States), European Medicines Agency (EMA, European Union), Medicines and Healthcare Products Regulatory Agency (MHRA, UK), Therapeutic Goods Administration (TGA, Australia), Health Canada (Canada), Pharmaceuticals and Medical Devices Agency (PMDA, Japan) and Central Drugs Standard Control Organization (CDSCO, India).

It was observed that regulatory guidelines differ with respect to territorial requirements; this demanded the need for universal harmonisation. Thus, **The International Council for Harmonization of Technical Requirements for Registration of Pharmaceuticals for Human**

Use (ICH) was founded in 1990 by united efforts of the United States, Europe and Japan to bring together different regulatory bodies globally and set ICH Guidelines for pharmaceutical drug product development. Since its inception, the ICH has evolved gradually with a mission to attain better harmonisation towards development and registration of medicines with a higher degree of safety, efficacy and quality worldwide. Although ICH has harmonised the drug regulatory aspects worldwide, the regional regulatory bodies continue to play a pivotal role in drug approvals across the territory.

Role of Drug Regulatory Affairs Department:

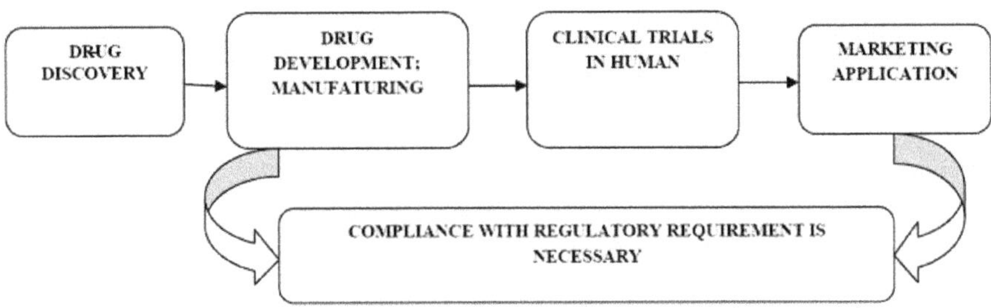

Fig 3.1 : Regulation fo Drug approval process

A. In Development phase -

- Ensuring that the legislative requirements are met -
- Recruit Scientific Advice - authorities
- Advice on development studies to demonstrate safety, quality and efficacy parameters.
- Set up regulatory strategy.
- Participate in cross-functional project teams
- Ensure application of guidelines for clinical trials.
- Submission of application to conduct clinical trials.
- Managing the regulatory submission -- Minimize time to market (every day counts!)
- Advice on a global development plan
- Optimize submission strategies -

  - Dossier preparation
  - Format, document re-uses
  - Electronic submissions
  - Review high-level documents/reports

- Interact with commercial side of business such as pricing and reimbursement.

B. In approval phase -

- Check progress of evaluation and anticipate questions.
- Clarify raised questions, plan response and strategies with other departments.
- Plan and manage agency meetings/hearings.
- Negotiate approval and Product Information with agencies.

C: In post approval phase -

- Compliance
- Submission of variations/amendments
- Renewals
- Pharmacovigilance
- Product information review
- New indications / new formulations
- Regulatory input to development plans/ Regulatory Intelligence

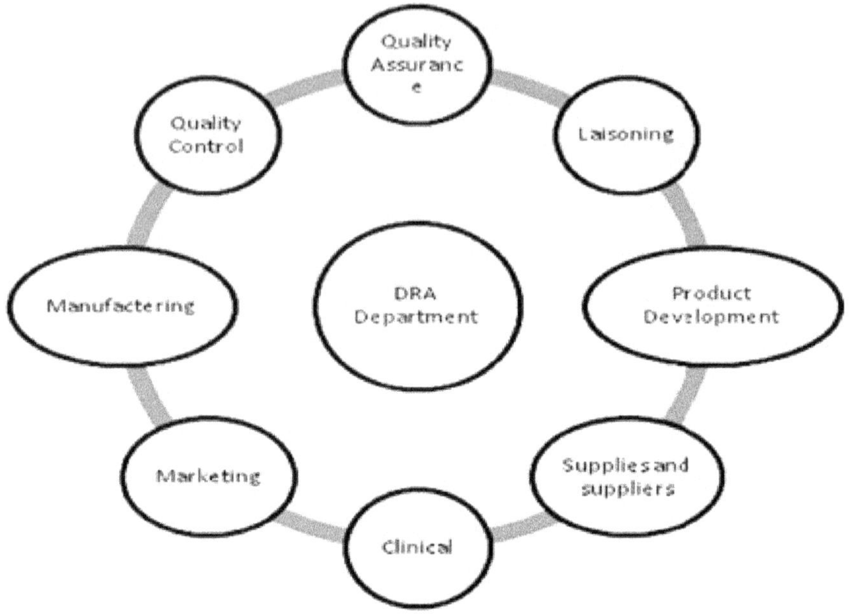

Fig 3.2 : Various Role of Drug Regulatory Affairs Department

Responsibility of the Regulatory Affairs Professionals -

Ø Ensuring that their companies comply with all of the regulations and laws pertaining to their business.

Ø Working with federal, state and local regulatory agencies and personnel on specific issues related to their business.

Ø Advising companies on the regulatory aspects and climate that would affect their proposed activities.

Ø Keep in touch with international legislation, guidelines and customer practices. Ø Keep up to the date with a company's product range.

Ø Collect, collate, and evaluate the scientific data that their research and development colleagues are generating.

Ø Formulate regulatory strategies for all appropriate regulatory submissions such as domestic, international and/or contract projects.

Ø Coordinate, prepare and review all appropriate documents for example dossier and submit them to regulatory authorities within a specified time frame in conjugation with the organization.

Ø Prepare and review of SOPs related to RA. Review of BMR, MFR, change control and other relevant documents.

Ø Monitor the progress of all registration submission.

Ø Maintain approved applications and the record of registration fees paid against submission of DMF's and other documents.

Ø Respond to queries and ensure that registration/ approval are granted without delay.

Ø Participate in R&D training, Pilot plant Scale Up, and Post Marketing Surveillance (ADR).

Ø Manage and review audit reports and compliance, regulatory and customer inspections.

Ø Provide accurate and complete information about the quality, safety and effectiveness of the product to the physicians and other healthcare professionals.

Regulatory requirements for drug approval:

Drug Development Teams - Most pharmaceutical and biotechnology firms employ drug development project teams to guide the processes involved in early drug discovery phase, through the various drug development stages and finally making the drug candidate into a therapeutic product.

The drug development team includes a diverse group of individuals with different philosophies and approaches to the development process. All team members must work closely together to ensure that a drug is both safe and efficacious.

The responsibilities of these project teams include -

1. Reviewing research results from experiments conducted by any of the various scientific disciplines.

2. Integrating new research results with previously generated data.

3. Planning research studies to further characterize a drug candidate.

4. Preparing a detailed drug development plan, including designation of key points or development milestones, generating a timeline for completion, and defining the critical path.

5. Monitoring the status of research studies to ensure that they are being conducted according to the timeline and critical path in the development plan and, if appropriate, modifying the plan as new information becomes available.
6. Comparing research results and development status and timelines with drug candidates under development by competitors.
7. Conducting appropriate market surveys to ensure that the development of a drug candidate is economically justified and continues to meet a medical need.
8. Reporting the status of the drug development program to management and making recommendations on the continued development of the drug candidate.

Drug development teams consist of following group of teams -

1. Discovery/development Team - The discovery and development groups are comprised of the basic scientists and chemists who created the new molecule. This group synthesizes drug substances for "drug-screening," pharmacology, and toxicology studies, and also prepares clinical supplies.
2. Nonclinical pharmacology and toxicology Team - This group studies the drug product in animal models for efficacy and safety in order to identify potential efficacy and safety issues in humans. It is critical for the clinical and development groups to work closely with the lexicologists in the design of animal studies to ensure their relevance to the clinical environment.
3. Clinical research Team - Clinical research has the ultimate responsibility for testing drug products in humans: the monitoring of drug safety rests squarely on the shoulders of clinical research. Clinical trials must be science-based with proper statistical methodologies and have clinically relevant end points. Clinical research interacts directly with the FDA and is responsible for the generation of study reports with input from biostatisticians and regulatory affairs. Clinical research can also generate the publications necessary for the marketing of any drug product.
4. Regulatory affairs Team - The regulatory affairs department is the interface with the FDA. It is their responsibility to ensure compliance with the rules and regulations established by the Federal Food Drug and Cosmetic Act and its amendments.

5. Marketing Team - The marketing group has the ultimate responsibility for marketing and selling the drug. As a result, they need product, labeling that differentiates their drug from those already marketed. Marketing has to provide creative concepts for the prescribing physician, the patient, and the company's senior management. They also have to make sure that, budget goals arc met. It is not uncommon for the marketing group to have differences of opinion from both the clinical and regulatory groups within their own company, as well as with the FDA.
6. Legal Team - In order for a drug to be financially successful, patent protection is a key element. The legal group must submit patents at the appropriate time and do all in its power to avoid lawsuits from potential competitors. The legal group also ensures that neither the FDA nor the other organization or company will challenge advertising and promotional materials.
7. **Management Team** – They co-ordinate with all the respective teams and responsible for successful completion of project in a time bound manner.

Pharmaceutical Drug Development:

- Pharmaceutical Drug Development is a process of bringing a newly synthesized drug molecule to the market once a lead compound has been identified through the process of drug discovery.

- These newly synthesized drug molecules which also known as New chemical entities (NCEs) or as New molecular entities (NMEs) are identified as Lead compound if they show promising pharmacological activity against a particular biological target that play a major role for a particular disease.

- The Identification of lead compound is carried out in drug discovery phase by means of suitable screening techniques such as High-throughput Screening.

- Drug Development process consist of a number of events that took place between the discovery of Lead compound to its eventual marketing.

- Broadly, the process of drug development can be divided into pre-clinical/non clinical and clinical phases.

- **Pre-clinical or Non- clinical Phase of Drug Development:** Pre-clinical Drug Development involves pharmacological and toxicological assessment of the potential new drug in animal models in order to establish its safety and efficacy before the administration to human volunteers in clinical trial phase.
- Pharmacological and toxicological assessment of the potential drug candidate is carried out by both in-vitro and in-vivo methods and in accordance with the guidelines of good laboratory practice (GLP). The GLP regulations are found in - 21 CFR Part 58.1: Good Laboratory Practice for Nonclinical Laboratory Studies.
- Cell lines or isolated tissues are used as in-vitro models and both rodent and non rodent animals such as mice, rat, guinea pig, dog, monkey etc are used as animal models for in-vivo testing.
- Such preclinical studies can be take up to 2 years to complete.

O Pre-clinical Drug Development involves following major type of studies –

1. **Pharmacological studies -**

i. **Pharmacokinetic profile Study** – It deals with study of ADME. Generally, ADME studies are conducted in two species, usually rats and dogs, repeated with different dose levels in males & females.

The main task of pharmacokinetic studies is to find an optimal dose level and to provide information about the dose-effect relationship. Therefore, different processes in the body are investigated and intensive information about the absorption, distribution, metabolism and excretion (ADME) of the substance is generated.

In vitro	*In vivo*	*In vivo*
1) Physical/chemical properties [lipophilicity (log P/log D), solubility, chemical stability (pKa)] 2) Metabolic stability 3) Hepatic clearance 4) Interaction between substances (inhibition/induction of CYPs) 5) Physiological characteristics (plasma protein/tissue binding) 6) Permeability 7) Plasmatic stability and total blood/plasma partition	1) Pharmacokinetic profile (concentration versus time) - Area under the curve - C_{max} - T_{max} - Distribution - Clearance - Half-life time 2) Biodisponibility bioavailability 3) Linearity 4) Metabolization 5) Routes of excretion	1) Toxicokinetic - Pharmacokinetic profile (concentration versus time) - Area under the curve - C_{max} - T_{max} - Distribution - Clearance - Half-life time 2) Biodisponibility 3) Metabolization 4) Routes of excretion 5) Quantification of biological fluids, organs, tissues, excrements and expired air (when necessary)

Table 2- Recommended non-clinical assays of ADME/PK.

- **Metabolism Study:** The drug metabolism studies needed to characterize the fate (whether the compound is changed and to what) of a lead or drug candidate in the body. Metabolism studies carried out by both *in-vitro* and *in-vivo* methods.

The *in-vitro* experiments can be conducted in a variety of systems, including CYP450 isozymes (the enzymes responsible for most oxidative metabolism of drugs), microsomes, hepatocytes, or liver slices. Since hepatocytes contain both phase 1(oxidative, hydrolysis, and reduction) and phase 2 (conjugation) metabolism systems and can be relatively easily obtained from pharmacology and toxicology animal species and from humans, many researchers select this model for the first assessment of metabolism. If the results from hepatocytes show extensive metabolism, additional *in-vitro* experiments are usually conducted first in microsomes to ascertain if oxidative metabolism is present and then in isolated CYP450 isozymes to determine which enzyme or enzymes are responsible.

For *in-vivo* metabolism studies in animal models, the selected animal species have metabolism profile that is similar to humans. Drug metabolism experiments in animal species used or to be used in toxicology studies are conducted using an appropriately labeled compound, usually a radioactive isotope such as carbon-14. Sometimes, drug metabolism studies are conducted with a less than desirable radiolabel isotope, such as 125I or 3H.

For more reliable results, the radiolabeled compound should be radiochemically pure and stable and have a specific activity high enough to be measurable after dosing. Also, the label needs to be in a position where it does not affect the physical, chemical, or pharmacological properties of the candidate and is not lost during phase 1 (oxidation, reduction, cleavage) or phase 2 (conjugation) metabolism.

The total radioactivity minus the parent compound concentration (determined by the bioanalytical assay method) in a specimen (plasma, serum, urine, bile), estimates the amount of metabolites present. If the difference is minimal and does not change over time, the extent of metabolism is low. For plasma or serum specimens, a small difference indicates that metabolites are not present in systemic circulation. For bile or urine specimens, high levels of radioactivity suggest a primary route of elimination for the parent and metabolites. Study of metabolite profile in urine and bile carried out to determine the amount of each potential metabolite. When the level of a metabolite is high, i.e., greater than 5% of the parent compound, attempts to isolate and identify the metabolite should be undertaken and metabolite's pharmacological and toxicological activity are evaluated.

i. **Pharmacodynamic profle Study** – Pharmacodynamic studies deal more specifically with followings-

   a. **Primary pharmacodynamic (PD) study** - Study Physiological effects of drug

   b. **Secondary pharmacodynamic study** - Study Mechanism of drug action and effects of the relevant compound which are not related to its desired therapeutic target.

   c. **Safety pharmacology studies** - Safety pharmacology studies are conducted to identify possible undesirable pharmacodynamic effects of a compound on selected physiological functions which may have an impact on human safety. Three types of safety pharmacology studies are performed which are as follows:

- **Core battery study** - The core battery of safety pharmacology studies which should be conducted in accordance with GLP is mandatory in order to investigate before first administration in humans. The core battery implies organ systems which are important with respect to life-supporting functions and are therefore most critical for life. This includes the cardiovascular, respiratory and central nervous system. Thereby, in vitro studies on isolated tissue, cells, receptors, ion channels or enzymes are an initial method to investigate potential pharmacological effects in concentration ranges of the respective substance on which an effect seems probable. For subsequent in vivo studies, the expected clinical route of administration should be used and the animals should ideally not be under anesthesia.

Safety pharmacology studies are normally performed by a single dose administration, whereby the exposure should at least be similar or even higher than the potential therapeutic concentration in humans.

b. **Follow-up studies** - The follow-up studies for the core battery may provide a deeper insight into kinetic conditions and potential repeat dose administrations on a suitable animal species.
c. **Supplemental studies** - In supplemental safety pharmacology studies organ systems not addressed in the core battery are investigated. This is notably done with other major organ systems such as the gastrointestinal, renal or the immune system.

1. **Toxicological Studies** - Toxicology defines the preclinical part of the safety assessment during drug development. By conducting toxicity studies, possible hazards and risks are identified.

i. Acute toxicity (Single dose) and Chronic toxicity (Repeated-dose) study –

  - Acute toxicity is usually assessed by administration of a single high dose of the test drug to rodents. Both rat and mice (male and female) are usually employed.
  - The single dose is administered by at least two routes, one of which should be the proposed route to be used in human beings. Animals are observed for overt effects and mortality up to 2 weeks and LD50

value is determined at 95% confidence level.

- **Repeated-dose** toxicity studies should be carried out in at least two species, out of which one should be a non-rodent. For **Repeated-dose** toxicity study small doses of drug administered 7 days a week up to 6 – 9 months.
- At least three dose levels should be used; the highest dose should produce observable toxicity, the lowest dose should not produce observable toxicity, but should be comparable to the intended therapeutic dose in humans; the intermediate dose should produce some symptoms, but not gross toxicity or death, and may be placed logarithmically between the other two doses. Observations should include body weights, clinical signs, clinical chemistries, hematology, and detailed histopathological changes in cells and tissues that occurred due to toxicity.

ii. **Reproductive toxicity study** – These studies evaluate male and female fertility, embryo and fetal death, parturition and the newborn, the lactation process, care of the young, and the potential teratogenicity of the drug candidate.

Historically, these reproductive parameters have been evaluated in three types of studies, generally referred to as **segment I, segment II, and segment III.**

Segment I, evaluates fertility and general reproductive performance in rats.

Segment II, commonly conducted in rats and rabbits, determines the embryo toxicity or teratogenic effects of the drug candidate.

Segment III, designated the perinatal and postnatal study and normally conducted only in rats, assesses the effects of the drug candidate on late fetal development, labor and delivery, lactation, neonatal viability, and growth of the newborn. Other rodents and nonrodent species, such as mice, guinea pigs, mini pigs, ferrets, hamsters, dogs, and nonhuman primates, have been used to evaluate the reproductive toxicity of drug candidates.

In Segment I, male fertility is determined by premating dosing of at least 4 weeks and with dosing continuing throughout the mating period. Histopathology of these tests and sperm analysis is used to detect effects on spermatogenesis. Female fertility is determined by premating dosing of at least 14 days with dosing continuing during the mating period.

Segment II, or Teratology studies, are designed to ascertain if a drug candidate has potential for embryotoicity or teratogenic effects and are conducted in a rodent and nonrodent species. The drug candidate is administered during the period of organogenesis, which is usually considered gestation day 6 to 15 for mice and rats and gestation day 6 to 18 for rabbits. Fetuses are delivered by Cesarean section a day or two before anticipated parturition. For rats, half of the fetuses are examined for visceral alterations and the other half are evaluated for skeletal abnormalities. For rabbits, microdissection techniques for soft tissue alterations allow all of the fetuses to be examined for both soft tissue and skeletal abnormalities.

Segment III studies are usually conducted only in rats and are designed to evaluate effects on perinatal and postnatal development of pups and on maternal function. The drug candidate is administered to the dams from implantation to the end of lactation. At the time of weaning, normally one male and one female offspring per litter are selected for rearing to adulthood and mating to assess reproductive competence.

iii. **Genotoxicity / Mutagenicity Study** – Mutagenicity study aim to determine whether the proposed drug is capable of inducing DNA damage, either by inducing alterations in chromosomal structure or by promoting changes in nucleotide base sequence. Mutagenicity studies are usually carried out by both in vitro and in vivo methods. The standard battery of tests recommended by ICH consists of a gene mutation assay in bacteria, an in vitro test of chromosomal damage, or an in vitro mouse lymphoma thymidine kinase (TK) assay, and an in vivo test of chromosomal damage using rodent hematopoietic cells.

Genetic toxicology test	Purpose
Ames bacterial mutation assay	Gene mutation in bacteria
Mouse lymphoma assay (MLA) Chinese hamster ovary (CHO) chromosomal aberration assay	In vitro evaluation of chromosomal damage
Micronucleus test (MNT)	Evaluation of in vivo chromosomal damage in bone marrow polychromatic erythrocytes

Table 3- Standard Genetic Toxicology Test Battery (ICH)

iii. **Carcinogenicity Study** –Long-term carcinogenicity study is carried out, particularly if the drug is used for administration over prolonged period (≥ 6 months). In such type of study animal is observed for the development of tumors. Carcinogenicity studies are conducted in two rodent species (mostly rats and mice) over a long-term period of 2 years. Two types of dose is used for the study – 1. Maximum tolerated dose (MTD) and 2. 25-fold AUC ratio (25:1 exposure ratio of rodent to human plasma AUC of the parent compound)

iv. **Immunotoxicity Study** –Ability of the drug compound to induce immune response or sensitivity is studied. Immunotoxicity which may be investigated during repeated dose toxicity studies. It identifies adverse effects of drugs on the immune system as immunosuppression which can lead to infectious diseases or malignancies, hypersensitivity or autoimmune reactions to self antigens. To determine potential immune reactions, different parameters like antibodies (IgM, IgE, IgG, etc.) are quantified, lymph nodes are weighed or lymphoid cell morphology is analyzed.

v. **Toxicokinetic Studies** – Toxicokinetic studies may be an integral part of nonclinical toxicity studies or may be conducted as separate, supportive studies. In general, toxicokinetic studies should be performed according to GLP regulations in conjunction with drug safety studies.

The primary objective of toxicokinetics studies is to define systemic exposure in animals along with the relationship of such exposure to the dose level and time course of the toxicity study. Secondarily, kinetic analyses relate exposure to toxicology findings and contribute to the assessment of the relevance of these findings to clinical safety.

In toxicokinetic studies, the matrix of choice (e.g., blood, plasma, excreta, or tissues) should be sampled frequently enough to permit estimation of the exposure without interfering with normal conduct of the study or causing undue physiologic stress to the animals. The doses and duration chosen for toxicokinetic evaluations should be based on those used in the single- and multiple-dose toxicology studies.

O Investigational New Drug Application

- After the successful completion of preclinical research, Drug developer or sponsor, must submit an Investigational New Drug (IND) application to respective regulatory authority such as FDA in US, CDSCO in India etc in order to start clinical research.
- The IND filing is the formal process by which a sponsor requests approval for testing of a drug in human subjects.

In the IND application, following things are must included:

- Animal study data and toxicity data
- Manufacturing information
- Clinical protocols (study plans) for studies to be conducted
- Data from any prior human research
- Information about the investigator
- Any additional data

After submitting IND, respective regulatory authority reviewed all the data and if satisfied, they grant the sponsor to begin clinical trial. It will take 30 -60 days after IND submission to get approval for clinical trial from the FDA.

The Investigator's Brochure: The Investigator's Brochure (IB) is an important document, not only required as a part of the IND but also prepared for presentation to potential clinical investigators and ultimately for presentation to the investigator's IRB(Institutional Review Board or Independent Review Board). The IB is a compilation of the clinical and nonclinical data on the investigational product that is relevant to the study of the product in human subjects.

Its purpose is to provide the investigators and others involved in the trial with information to facilitate their understanding of the rationale for, and their compliance with, many key features of the protocol, such as the dose, dose frequency/interval, methods of administration, and safety monitoring procedurcs.

The IB also provides insight to support the clinical management of the study subjects during the course of the clinical trial. The information should be presented in a concise, simple, objective, and nonpromotional form that enables a clinician or potential investigator to understand it and make his or her own unbiased risk-benefit assessment of the appropriateness of the proposed trial. For this reason, a medically qualified person should generally participate in the editing of an IB, but the contents of the IB should be approved by the disciplines that generated the described data.

The IB should be reviewed at least annually and revised as necessary in compliance with a sponsor's written procedures.

Generally, the sponsor is responsible for ensuring that an up-to-date IB is made available to the investigator(s), and the investigators are responsible for providing the upto- date IB to the responsible IRBs.

The following provides the information that should be included in the IB –

1. **Title Page** - This should provide the sponsor's name, the identity of each investigational product (i.e., research number, chemical or approved generic name, and trade name(s) where legally permissible and desired by the sponsor), and the release date. It is also suggested that an edition number and a reference to the number and date of the edition it supersedes be provided.

TITLE PAGE OF INVESTIGATOR'S BROCHURE (Example)

- Sponsor's Name: Product: Research Number: Name(s): Chemical, Generic (if approved)
- Trade Name(s) (if legally permissible and desired by the sponsor) Edition Number:
- Release Date:
- Replaces Previous Edition Number:
- Date:

2. **Confidentiality Statement** - The sponsor may wish to include a statement instructing the investigator/ recipients to treat the IB as a confidential document for the sole information and use of the investigator's team and the IRB/IEC.

3. **Contents of the Investigator's Brochure** - The IB should contain the following sections, each with literature references where appropriate:

1. Table of Contents
2. Summary
3. Introduction
4. Physical, Chemical, and Pharmaceutical Properties and Formulation
5. Nonclinical Studies

    1. Nonclinical Pharmacology
    2. Pharmacokinetics and Product Metabolism in Animals
    3. Toxicology

6. Effects in Humans

    1. Pharmacokinetics and Product Metabolism in Humans
    2. Safety and Efficacy
    3. Marketing Experience

7. Summary of Data and Guidance for the Investigator
8. Publications
9. Reports (these references should be found at the end of each chapter.) and Appendices (if any)

O **Clinical Phase of Drug Development:** Pre-clinical research provides a basic idea about drug's safety in animal models, but it is not a substitute for human subjects. "Clinical research" refers to studies, or trials, that involve human subjects to establish the safety and efficacy of drug.

Clinical trials consist of 4 phases –

Phase I –

- **Study Participants:** 20 to 100 healthy volunteers
- **Length of Study:** Several months to one year
- Purpose:Safety and Dose range

Phase II –

- **Study Participants:** 100 to 300 volunteers with the disease.

- **Length of Study:** Up to 2 years
- Purpose: Safety and Efficacy

Phase III-

- **Study Participants:** 300 to 3,000 volunteers who have the target disease
- **Length of Study:** 1 to 4 years
- Purpose: Confirm Efficacy and long term Safety, monitoring of adverse reactions

O New Drug Application (NDA)

- After the successful completion of clinical research, if the drug candidate proven satisfactory to be safe and effective for its intended use, then drug sponsor can submit New Drug Application (NDA) to respective regulatory authority in order to get marketing license and start commercial production.
- To submit New Drug Application (NDA) filing, drug sponsor must provide all the research data which are obtained from preclinical to Phase 3 clinical trial along with following documents –
- Proposed labeling
- Safety updates
- Drug abuse information
- Patent information
- Location where the clinical trial studies have been conducted
- compliance Report of preclinical study
- Directions for use

NDA Review - After NDA received by the regulatory agency, it undergoes a technical screening. This evaluation ensures that sufficient data and information have been submitted in each area that justify NDA filing.

At the conclusion of the review of NDA, there are 3 possible outcomes that can send to drug sponsor:

1. Not approvable- it display list of deficiencies and explain the cause of rejection.
2. Approvable – minor changes are suggested for the marketing approval
3. Approved for marketing.

It will take 6 – 12 months after NDA submission to get approval letter for marketing

- **Phase IV** –Phase IV trials are post-approval trials in which adverse drug reactions (ADRs) are monitored to ensure drug's safety after being marketed. It is also called post-marketing surveillance studies. These studies carried out by drug sponsor, government agency or individual research organizations periodically after the drug being marketed.

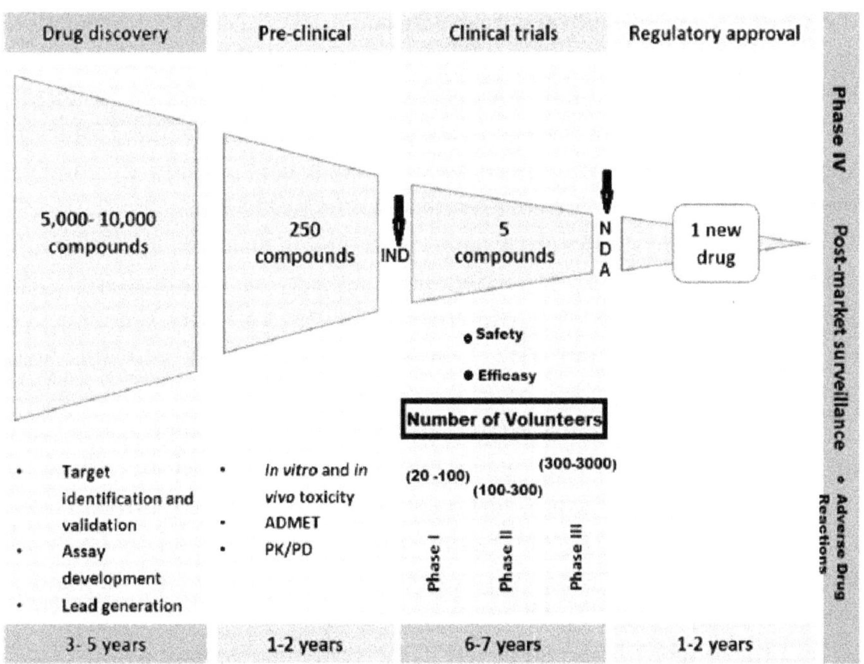

Figure 3.2 : Different Phases o drug development

O BE Study - Bioequivalence (BE) studies are performed to demonstrate that different formulations or regimens of drug product are similar to each other in terms of their therapeutic benefit (efficacy) and non therapeutic side effects (safety). They play a key and pivotal role in the drug development process by ensuring that when a patient switches to a new formulation in the marketplace, safety and efficacy will be maintained.

Bioequivalence studies are primarily used by pharmaceutical sponsors of new drug entities to demonstrate that the formulation used in Phase III confirmatory clinical trials is sufficiently similar to the final commercial formulation to be marketed following approval.

BE studies can be viewed as providing necessary and sufficient reassurance to regulators that the formulation to be marketed is the same as that used in the clinical confirmatory trials without the need to repeat the development program or to perform a therapeutic equivalence study in patients with clinical endpoints .

Bioequivalence studies must also be performed following substantial postmarketing formulation alteration. They are also used by what is termed the 'generic' pharmaceutical industry to gain market access for formulations of established drug therapies when the patent of the original sponsor's formulation expires. When the original sponsors themselves perform a formulation change (for instance, change the site of manufacture) following approval, they often also must do a bioequivalence study to convince regulators that the new formula is safe and effective to market

Bioequivalence studies are usually conducted in male and female healthy volunteer subjects. Each individual subject is administered two formulations (T=Test or R=Reference) in one of two sequences of treatments (e.g., RT and TR), R is the 'standard' and T is the 'new' formulation.

Each administration is separated by a washout period appropriate to the drug under study; this washout period consists of five half-lives between administrations. Half-life is determined by looking at the elimination (after Cmax) part of the PK concentration versus time curve and is simply the length of time it takes the body to eliminate one-half of the amount of whatever drug is in the body at any given time. In general, if five half- lives go by, little to no drug should be left in the systemic circulation.

Sequence Group	Period			Number of Subjects
	1	Washout	2	
1(RT)	R	—	T	$n/2$
2(TR)	T	—	R	$n/2$
R=Reference, T=Test				

Figure 3.3: Schematic Plan of a 2 × 2 Cross-over Study

Such a design is termed a 2 × 2 cross-over [237] and is a type of design typically applied in bioequivalence trials.

To demonstrate equivalence in plasma concentration profiles, rate and extent of bioavailability of the drug substance in plasma must be sufficiently similar so as to meet the regulatory standard for showing that exposure of the body to the drug substance is the same between formulations. For this purpose, Cmax (rate) and AUC (extent) are typically used as summary measures for the plasma concentration curves and are required to be demonstrated as equivalent under preset decision rules to achieve regulatory approval.

O Clinical Trial Protocol:The clinical trial protocol is a document that describes how a clinical trial will be conducted (the objective(s), design, methodology, statistical considerations and organization of a clinical trial,) and ensures the safety of the trial subjects and integrity of the data collected. Clinical trials carried out in accordance with the guidelines of Good Clinical Practice (GCP) and ICH. The GCP-ICH regulations are found in - **E6 (R2) Good Clinical Practice: Integrated Addendum to ICH E6 (R1).**

The contents of a trial protocol should generally include the following topics

1.

General Information

1. Protocol title, protocol identifying number, and date. Any amendment(s) should also bear the amendment number(s) and date(s).
2. Name and address of the sponsor and monitor (if other than the sponsor).
3. Name and title of the person(s) authorized to sign the protocol and the protocol amendment(s) for the sponsor.
4. Name, title, address, and telephone number(s) of the sponsor's medical expert for the trial.
5. Name and title of the investigator(s) who is (are) responsible for conducting the trial, and the address and telephone number(s) of the trial site(s).
6. Name, title, address, and telephone number(s) of the qualified physician (or dentist, if applicable), who is responsible for all trial-site related medical (or dental) decisions (if other than investigator).
7. Name(s) and address(es) of the clinical laboratory(ies) and other medical and/or technical department(s) and/or institutions involved in the trial.

2.

Background Information

1. Name and description of the investigational product(s).
2. A summary of findings from nonclinical studies that potentially have clinical significance and are relevant to the trial.
3. Summary of the known and potential risks and benefits, if any, to human subjects.
4. Description of and justification for the route of administration, dosage, dosage regimen, and treatment period(s).

5. A statement that the trial will be conducted in compliance with the protocol, GCP and the applicable regulatory requirement(s).
6. Description of the population to be studied.

7. References to literature and data that are relevant to the trial, and that provide background for the trial.

3.

Trial Objectives and Purpose -

A detailed description of the objectives and the purpose of the trial.

4. Trial Design

The scientific integrity of the trial and the credibility of the data from the trial depend substantially on the trial design.

A description of the trial design should include:

1. A specific statement of the primary endpoints and the secondary endpoints, if any, to be measured during the trial.
2. A description of the type/design of trial to be conducted (e.g. double-blind, placebo-controlled, parallel design) and a schematic diagram of trial design, procedures and stages.
3. A description of the measures taken to minimize/avoid bias, including: Randomization; Blinding.

4. A description of the trial treatment(s) and the dosage and dosage regimen of the investigational product(s). Also include a description of the dosage form, packaging, and labelling of the investigational product(s).
5. The expected duration of subject participation, and a description of the sequence and duration of all trial periods, including follow-up, if any.
6. A description of the "stopping rules" or "discontinuation criteria" for individual subjects, parts of trial and entire trial.
7. Accountability procedures for the investigational product(s), including the placebo(s) and comparator(s), if any.

8. Maintenance of trial treatment randomization codes and procedures for breaking codes.

9. The identification of any data to be recorded directly on the CRFs (i.e. no prior written or electronic record of data), and to be considered to be source data.

5.

Selection and Withdrawal of Subjects -

1. Subject inclusion criteria.

2. Subject exclusion criteria.

3. Subject withdrawal criteria (i.e. terminating investigational product treatment/trial treatment) and procedures specifying:

a. When and how to withdraw subjects from the trial/ investigational product treatment.

b. The type and timing of the data to be collected for withdrawn subjects.

c. Whether and how subjects are to be replaced.

d. The follow-up for subjects withdrawn from investigational product treatment/trial treatment.

6.

Treatment of Subjects -

1. The treatment(s) to be administered, including the name(s) of all the product(s), the dose(s), the dosing schedule(s), the route/mode(s) of administration, and the treatment period(s), including the follow-up period(s) for subjects for each investigational product treatment/ trial treatment group/arm of the trial.

2. Medication(s)/treatment(s) permitted (including rescue medication) and not permitted before and/or during the trial.
3. Procedures for monitoring subject compliance.

7.

Assessment of Efficacy -

1. Specification of the efficacy parameters.
2. Methods and timing for assessing, recording, and analysing of efficacy parameters.

8.

Assessment of Safety -

1. Specification of safety parameters.
2. The methods and timing for assessing, recording, and analysing safety parameters.
3. Procedures for eliciting reports of and for recording and reporting adverse event and intercurrent illnesses.
4. The type and duration of the follow-up of subjects after adverse events.

9.

Statistics -

1. A description of the statistical methods to be employed, including timing of any planned interim analysis.
2. The number of subjects planned to be enrolled. In multicentre trials, the numbers of enrolled subjects projected for each trial site should be specified. Reason for the choice of sample size including clinical

justification.

3. The level of significance to be used.

4. Criteria for the termination of the trial.

5. Procedure for accounting for missing, unused, and spurious data.

6. Procedures for reporting any deviation(s) from the original statistical plan (any deviation(s) from the original statistical plan should be described and justified in protocol and/or in the final report, as appropriate).

7. The selection of subjects to be included in the analyses (e.g. all randomized subjects, all dosed subjects, all eligible subjects, evaluable subjects).

10.

Direct Access to Source Data/Documents -

The sponsor should ensure that it is specified in the protocol or other written agreement that the investigator(s)/institution(s) will permit trial-related monitoring, audits, IRB/IEC review, and regulatory inspection(s), providing direct access to source data/documents.

11.

Quality Control and Quality Assurance

12.

Ethics - *Description of ethical considerations relating to the trial.*

13.

Data Handling and Record Keeping

14.
__Financing and Insurance__- Financing and insurance if not addressed in a separate agreement.

15.
__Publication Policy__- Publication policy, if not addressed in a separate agreement.

16.
Supplements

O <u>Biostatistics in Pharmaceutical Product Development -</u>

Statistics plays an important role in drug product development. Its use is necessary for planning and analyzing trials and using statistics correctly is crucial for the success of drug development programs. Applications of biostatistics in pharmaceutical product development are as follows –

- Provide scientific method thinking into the target identification process
- Assess the ability to Quantify effect on target of interest
    - Does animal model translate into human?
    - How will effective dose be identified?
- Provide critical input into quantification of risk (Risk assessment)
- Agree criteria for stopping dose escalation
- Assist in establishing go/no go decision criteria (significance testing-p value)
- Review of safety margins from animal data
- Assist in appropriate study design selection and of Primary endpoints for studies.
- Design and implementation of randomization systems in study design.
- Helps in sample collection, data analysis and refinement, error and bias detection.

- Design and optimize formulation, optimize process parameters in pilot plant scale up.
- Used as Analytical methods validation tool.

Key Statistical supports in different phases of drug development are summarize below –

Milestones	Activities	Statistical support
Nominate an API for clinical development	Discover the API and perform various preclinical studies	Multiple comparison techniques for combinatorial chemists; analysis of genomic data; design and analysis of animal safety studies, etc.
Perform Phase I clinical studies	Determine Phase I dosage type (e.g., liquid, capsule, tablet [or new technology])	Analysis of historical data; statistical thinking (design and analyze experiments)
	Excipient compatibility studies	Design and analyze experiments
	Accelerated stability studies	Regression analysis
Perform Phase IIA (dose ranging) and IIB (proof of concept) clinical studies	Determine Phase II dosage type (new technology)	Analysis of historical data; statistical thinking (design and analyze experiments)
	Evaluate excipient compatibility (if not performed previously)	Design and analyze experiments
	Develop Phase II dosage formulation	Design and analyze factorial and/or mixture experiments
	Develop Phase II manufacturing process	Design and analyze factorial and/or response surface experiments
Perform Phase III clinical studies	(If necessary, determine Phase III dosage type)	(Design and analyze experiments to investigate scalability and/or economic concerns with Phase II dosage type)
	Develop and/or scale Phase III dosage formulation	Design and analyze factorial and/or mixture experiments
	Develop and/or scale Phase III manufacturing process	Design and analyze factorial, mechanistic, and/or response surface experiments
	Develop PAT applications	Multivariate analysis
	Transfer technology to commercial manufacturing division	Write reports and consult
Submit new-drug application	Develop and/or scale commercial formulation and process	Design and analyze factorial, mechanistic, mixture, and/or response surface experiments
	Define design and knowledge spaces for DP formulation and process	Design and analyze product- and process-understanding experiments
	Conduct ICH campaign	Analyze ICH stability studies (set expiry)
Milestones	Activities	Statistical support
Produce commercial product	Establish QA procedures	Assess process capability and establish quality systems to control the process (SPC, PAT, establish sampling plans, etc.)
	Monitor DP stability	Analyze data from annual stability lots
	Improve the process	Data mining, DoE, Six Sigma techniques, Lean techniques, JIT manufacturing, etc.

Table 4 - Drug Product Development and Statistical Support

O Data Presentation for FDA Submissions:

Following points to be consider for NDA submissions or other regulatory submissions –

1. TEXT EXPOSITION –

A. **Content** - Most NDA submissions contain an enormous amount of data, which cannot be presented entirely within the body of a document. Although all the data collected for an individual subject or patient (or groups of subjects or patients) may be important, critical judgment must be exercised in the selection of key data for presentation and discussion within a given document. Data necessary for the development of a specific thesis should be presented within the body of the document rather than placed into a remote appendix, which will impede the review.

Less important data can be summarized briefly, clearly referenced in text, and placed in appendices. Any data submitted will have to be evaluated, so the inclusion of extraneous data will slow the review of the application. The submission should note the existence of such data and have it available upon request of the FDA.

B. **Tone** - The tone of the text should be formal without being stilted. Avoid legal language on the one hand and colloquial or informal language on the other.

C. **Conciseness** - The following points address ways of making NDA documents more concise.

   1. Keep the language simple and straightforward.
   2. Use acronyms and initialisms to speed up the flow of text if they are easily recognized and have been spelled out at first mention. Those that may be confused with another used in the same document should be spelled out.
   3. Eliminate redundancies. A careful review of the text will find many words, phrases, and even sentences that can be omitted. Sentences can often be combined by the deletion of redundant phrases, thus

improving the flow of the text.

D. **Correctness** - The textual presentation should agree with the tabular data in the document; in turn, the tabular data should agree with the data source (which agrees with the case report for and other clinical documentation). This is critical to the scientific merit of the submission. When lack of agreement between in- text data and source documents is found, the entire submission may be suspect, and the reviewer will be inclined to spend much more time evaluating the raw data to be sure of the conclusions.

E. **Consistency** - Consistent punctuation, capitalization, abbreviations, and other styling conventions are much desired in all documents with proper judgment.

F. **Clarity** -The FDA reviewer should be able to read through an application expeditiously and not have to stop to try to discern the meaning of a textual presentation. Clarity is facilitated by careful attention to the following:

1. Punctuation.
2. Sentence structure and length.
3. Misplaced modifiers.
4. Parallelism. Because much of the data in an NDA involves comparisons of one group to another, parallel structure is important in presenting the data.

I. **Outline of Sections and Subsections** - The clear relationship of one section to another is critical to the review of a document.

The decimal system is a very popular outlining system; it is easy to use and can be set up automatically in most current word processing software applications. Another popular outlining system is the alphanumeric system, where letters and numbers alternate as section headers.

H. **Indenting** - Avoid indenting large sections of text. Most text should be flush to the left margin with appropriate headers to identify the section. Multiple and sequential indenting wastes **of** space and is confusing. Short lists are appropriately indented, and conventions like indenting with bullets are useful to break up long sections of text.

A. Global to Specific -

For any section, begin with global statements or data and then discuss the specifics. For example, in the discussion of adverse events, the overall presentation of the events should precede the presentation by severity, by relationship, by subgroup, etc. It is particularly important in the discussion of the populations evaluated in a particular document. Begin with the all inclusive population first, then define the subpopulations.

2. TABULAR PRESENTATION -

In-text, tables should be used whenever they simplify the presentation and allow for substantial reduction in text. Comprehensive multipage tables that interrupt text should be avoided, if possible, unless they are critical. However, if the tables are very important, they can be placed in the same volume in an appendix. Usually, data can be collapsed to be included in the in-text table, with reference to the full table in an easy-to-locate appendix. It should be mentioned that any tables, figures, or graphs in the appendices must have in-text references. Information from the tables should not be repeated in the text except as part of a concluding statement about the tabular data or trends seen in the data. The commentary on data from the tables should precede the table, beginning with an introduction to the table by number and a statement identifying what type of data it contains.

Additional commentary related to the table but not derived from the tabular data may follow the table.

A. **Title** - All tables require concise but descriptive titles.

B. **Data Source** - Every table should identify the source of the data contained in it. This is usually done in a footnote to the table. The volume and page numbers will be inserted at the end of the project.

C. **Footnotes** - Footnotes should be assigned letters (superscripted), not symbols or numbers, which can be confused with the data. In multipage tables, footnotes should be assigned letters in the order in which they appear on the specific page of the table. Always begin such tables on a new page to avoid changing the footnotes as the tables shift with the addition of preceding text.

D. **Orientation** - Portrait tables are always preferable to landscape tables. If data appear not to fit in the portrait orientation, try changing the axes of the table, so that the axis with more individual descriptors is vertical, whereas the axis with fewer items is horizontal (column headings). Also consider revising the table into separate sections under the same column headers, with descriptive headings for each section spanning the width of the table.

E. **Order of Data Presentation** - In multiple tables with similar data, present the data in the same order as much as possible. If the first column always has the active drug and the second column the placebo or comparative agent, then keep this order throughout the tables. In the analysis of data by demographic or disease subgroup, it is helpful to keep the subgroup of concern

(i.e., women, the elderly, racial subgroups, impaired renal function) in the same column in each table.

F. **Present Meaningful Data Together** - Try to present the data that will be evaluated and compared as close together as possible rather than scattered around the table.

O Management of Clinical Trials – The key elements in managing clinical programs are as follows -.

* **Investigator selection** - US GCP Federal Regulations and ICH GCP Guidelines mandate that a sponsor select only investigators qualified by training and experience as appropriate experts to evaluate an investigational product (21 CFR 312.53). A similar reference appears in the ICH GCP Guidelines as well.

- **Preinvestigational site visits (PISV)** - After prescreening of potential investigators is established, it is vitally important that a PISV be conducted at the investigational site with the investigator and their staff to continue to assess their ability to conduct the trial. The PISV is usually performed by the monitor or an authorized individual appointed by the sponsor company.

***Study initiation visits (SIV)** – Once the PISV is complete, an SIV is the next step.The initiation visit is a training programme. This is the last training on the protocol that the investigators and their staffs will have before beginning to recruit and enroll subjects into the trial. During this meeting, the monitor will review the following in details – Study Protocol, Adverse experience and serious adverse experience reporting documentation,reports, Product dispensation and accountability, Case Report Form (CRF) completion, Review of regulatory documents and Source documentation.

***Trial conduct and execution** -There are several other key components to trial execution that will require special attention: subject recruitment, the informed consent, IRBs/IEC review product accountability, adverse experience and adverse reaction reporting, financial disclosure, and record retention. Each is critical in the overall success of a clinical trial.

- **Periodic monitoring visits** - Both the CFR and the ICH GCP guidelines require that the sponsor monitor the progress of the clinical trial at the site where the trial is being conducted. The overall purpose of these periodic monitoring visits by the sponsor's monitor is to assure that the investigators and their staffs follow GCP regulations and guidelines and adhere to the protocol to assure that the rights of the subjects participating in the clinical trial are being protected and that the data reported is complete, accurate, and verifiable.
- **Subject Recruitment**- One of the surest ways to decrease the overall time to complete a clinical trial is to recruit subjects into the trial in the shortest amount of time. The secret to effective subject recruitment is planning on how and where to recruit a subject population. In planning for recruitment, one must know and understand the subject population that will meet the protocol criteria. What motivates these subjects to participate in the clinical trial? What kind of medical treatment are they presently receiving, and who are they seeing to get this treatment? What is the present status of their medical condition?

***Product accountability** - Clinical trials evaluate new investigational drug/devices which have not yet received marketing authorization from the appropriate health care authority. Therefore it is mandatory that strict control be maintained on any investigational product. The investigator is responsible for the accountability of the test product. Investigational products should only be prescribed by the investigator or authorized sub investigators. The sponsor is responsible for retrieving/verifying the disposition of all used and unused product. Detailed records of product accountability must be maintained throughout a trial with information on the date dispensed, the quantity dispensed, the subject identifier (subject number), and the batch number of product prescribed.

***AE and ADR reporting** -Drug safety and adverse reactions are closely related in an inversely proportional manner. In the United States, drug safety is under strict legislative control mandated by the FDA. Federal regulations require a sponsor to report adverse experiences and reactions for an investigational product at both the investigational and the post marketing stages.

*Financial disclosure - One of the newest components of a clinical trial is financial disclosure. This regulation initiated in the United States on February 2, 1999, is required on all current or ongoing clinical trials filed in an IND. Financial disclosure is defined by the FDA as compensation related to the outcome of the study, proprietary interest in the product (e.g., patent), significant equity interest in the sponsor of the study, significant payments of other sorts to the investigator or institution (e.g., equipment, honorariums). The reason for this regulation is to assure the FDA that appropriate steps were taken to minimize bias in the design, conduct, reporting, and analysis of the studies even when the investigator has a financial interest in a new product.

***Study close-out visits (SCV)** - Once a trial is completed at an investigational site, the study must be appropriately closed. This cannot occur until all of the subjects have completed the course of the trial, or were dropped or withdrawn, and all data queries and issues have been addressed and resolved in the final evaluations. Only when this is done can the monitor proceed to a close-out visit. The following checklist will guide the monitor in completing the SCV:

All subjects entered in the trial have been accounted for.

All CRF pages have been completed and retrieved. All data queries have been resolved.

All AEs and ADRs have been reported and followed up.

All investigational product has been accounted for and disposed of or returned to the sponsor. All remaining supplies (CRFs, ancillary supplies) are returned or disposed of properly.

Regulatory records are complete and organized in the Trial Binder. All outstanding issues are addressed.

- **Records retention and inspections** - Record retention is critical to the ongoing viability of the study data. The FDA or other health care authorities may conduct an on-site inspection to verify the data from a given site at some time after submission of the New Drug Application (NDA). This information must be readily available at the site. Both the CFR and the ICH require that the records be retained for two years after the date of a marketing application is approved.

CHAPTER IV

TOTAL QUALITY MANAGEMENT

TOTAL QUALITY MANAGEMENT:

Total - made up of the whole

Quality - degree of excellence a product or service provides

Management - act, art, or manner of planning, controlling and Directing.

Therefore, TQM is the art of managing the whole to achieve excellence.

Characteristics of TQM

- Committed management.
- Adopting and communicating about total quality management.
- Closer customer relations.
- Closer provider relations.
- Benchmarking.
- Increased training.
- Open organization
- Employee empowerment.
- Flexible production.
- Process improvements.
- Process measuring

Principles of TQM

1. Produce quality work the first time and every time.
2. Focus on the customer.
3. Have a strategic approach to improvement.
4. Improve continuously.
5. Encourage mutual respect and teamwork

The key elements of the TQM

Focus on the customer.
Employee involvement
Continuous improvement

Focus on the customer

- It is important to identify the organization's customers.
- External customers consume the organization's product or service.
- Internal customers are employees who receive the output of other employees.
- Since the quality is considered the job of all employees, employees should be involved in quality initiatives.

- Front line employees are likely to have the closest contact with external customers and thus can make the most valuable contribution to quality.
- Therefore, employees must have the authority to innovate and improve quality.

Continuous Improvement

- The quest for quality is a never-ending process in which people are continuously working to improve the performance, speed, and number of features of the product or service.
- Continuous improvement means that small, incremental improvement that occurs on a regular basis will eventually add up to vast improvement in quality.
- TQM is the management process used to make continuous improvements to all functions.
- TQM represents an ongoing, continuous commitment to improvement.

- The foundation of total quality is a management philosophy that supports meeting customer requirements through continuous improvement.

Continuous Process Improvement

- View all work as process – production and business.
- Process – purchasing, design, invoicing, etc.
- Inputs – process – outputs.
- Process improvement – increased customer satisfaction.
- Improvement – 5 ways:
- reduce resources, reduce errors, meet expectations of downstream customers, make process safer, make process more satisfying to the person doing

Benefits Of TQM:

- Improved quality.
- Employee participation.
- Team work.
- Working relationships.
- Customer satisfaction.
- Employee satisfaction.
- Productivity.
- Communication.
- Profitability.
- Market share.

Importance of TQM in pharma industry Handling:

- Containers should be opened carefully and subsequently resealed in an approved manner.

- Highly sensitising material such as penicillins and cephalosporins should be handled in separate production areas.
- Highly active or toxic API (e.g. certain steroids, cytostatic substances) should be manufactured in a dedicated area and using dedicated equipment.
- Pure and final API should be handled in an environment giving adequate protection against contamination.

Storage:

- Secure storage facilities should be designated for use to prevent damage or deterioration of materials.
- These should be kept clean and tidy and subject to appropriate pest control measures.
- Environmental conditions should be recorded.
- The condition of stored material should be assessed at appropriate intervals.
- Storage conditions for api should be based upon stability studies considering time, temperature, humidity, light etc

Packaging:

- Labelling and packaging processes should be defined and controlled to ensure that correct packaging materials are used correctly, and other specified requirements are met.
- Printed labels should be securely stored to avoid mix-ups arising.
- Marking and labelling should be legible and durable, provide sufficient information, for accurate identification and indicate, if appropriate, required storage conditions, retest and/or expiry date.

Facilities and equipment:

- The location, design, and construction of buildings should be suitable for the type and stage of manufacture involved, protecting the product from contamination (including cross-contamination) and protecting operators and the environment from the product.
- Equipment surfaces in contact with materials used in api manufacture should be non- reactive.

Sterile area

- Personnel suffering from an infectious disease or having open lesions on the exposed surface of the body should avoid activities which could compromise the quality of API.
- Smoking, eating, drinking, chewing and storage of food should be restricted to designated areas separated from production or control areas.

Labelling

- Each container should be identified by an appropriate label, showing at least the product identification and the assigned batch code, or any other easily understandable combination of both.

- . Containers for external distribution may require additional labels.

Computerised systems :

- . Computer systems should be designed and operated to prevent unauthorised entries or changes to the programme.
- In the case of manual entry of quality critical data there should be a second independent check to verify accuracy of the initial entry.
- A back-up system should be provided of all quality critical data.

Advantages of tqm

- Improves reputation- faults and problems are spotted and sorted quicker.
- Higher employee morale- workers motivated by extra responsibility, teamwork and involvement indecisions of tqm.
- Lower cost.
- Decrease waste as fewer defective products and no need for separate.

Disadvantages of tqm:

- Initial introduction cost.
- Benefits may not be seen for several years.
- Workers may be resistant to change. A model for organization management.

BENEFITS OF TOTAL QUALITY MANAGEMENT

- Financial benefits include lower costs, higher returns on sales and investment, and the ability to charge higher rather than competitive prices.
- Improved access to global markets, higher customer retention levels, less
- Time required to develop new innovations, and a reputation as a quality firm.
- Total quality management (tqm) is one such approach that seeks to improve quality and
- Performance which will meet or exceed customer expectations.

CONCLUSION:

- TQM encourages participation amongst employees, managers, and organization as whole.
- Using Quality management reduces rework nearly to zero in an achievable goal .The responsibilities either its professional, social, legal one that rest with the pharmaceutical manufacturer for the assurance of quality of product are tremendous and it can only be achieved by well organised.
- Work culture and complete engagement of the employees at the workplace. It should be realised that national & international regulations must be implemented systematically and process.

- Control should be practiced rigorously.
- Thus quality is critically important ingredient to organisational success today which can be achieved by TQM, an organisational approach that focusses on quality as an over achieving goals, aimed at aimed at the prevention of defects rather than detection of defects..

QUALITY BY DESIGN(QbD)

Definition:

'Systematic approach to development that begins with predefined objectives and emphasizes product and process understanding and process control, based on sound science and quality risk.

The concept of QBD was mention in ICH Q8 guidelines, which states that, "To identify quality cannot be tested in products, i.e. Quality should be built into product by design.

Advantages:

- Benefits for Industry:
- Better understanding of the process.
- Less batch failure.
- More efficient and effective control of change.

Additional opportunities:

- Reduction of post-approval submissions.
- More efficient technology transfer to manufacturing.
- Risk-based approach and identification.
- Innovative process validation approaches.

Objectives:

- The main objectives of QBD is to ensure the quality products, for that product & process characteristics important to desired performance must be resulting from a combination of prior knowledge & new estimation during development.
- From this knowledge & data process measurement & desired attributes may be constructed.
- Ensures combination of product & process knowledge gained during development.

The Target Product Quality Profile (TPQP):

TPQP has been defined as a "prospective and dynamic summary of the quality characteristics of a drug product that ideally will be achieved to ensure that the desired quality, and thus the safety and efficacy, of a drug product is realized.

TPP forms the basis for product design in the following way

- Dosage form Route of administration
- Strength Release.
- Pharmacological characteristic
- Drug product quality criteria.
- Pharmaceutical elegance.

Critical Quality Attribute (CQA):

- Once TPQP has been identified, the next step is} to identify the relevant CQAs.
- A CQA has been defined as "a physical, chemical,} biological, or microbiological property or characteristic that should be within an appropriate limit, range, or distributed to ensure the desired product quality.
- Prior product knowledge, such as the} accumulated laboratory, nonclinical and clinical experience with a specific product-quality attribute, is the key in making these risk assessments.

Critical Process Parameter (CPPs) :

- Critical process parameters (CPPs) are defined as "parameters whose variability have an impact on a CQA and therefore should be monitored or controlled to ensure the process produces the desired quality.
- Process robustness is defined as the ability of a process to demonstrate acceptable quality and performance and tolerate variability in inputs at the same time.

Risk Assessment:

- Quality risk management is a systematic process for the assessment, control, communication, and review of risks to the quality of the drug (medicinal) product across the product lifecycle.
- The initial list of potential parameters which can affect CQAs can be quite extensive but can be reduced by quality risk assessment (QRA).

Design Space:

- The ICH Q8(R2) States that the design space is multi-dimensional combination and interaction of input variables (e.g., material attributes) and process parameters that have been demonstrated to provide assurance of quality.
- Working within the design space is not} considered as a change. Movement out of the design space is a change and would normally initiate a regulatory post approval change process.

Control Strategy:

- Control strategy is defined as "a planned set of controls, derived from current product and process understanding that assures process performance and product quality".
- The ability to evaluate and ensure the quality of in process and/or final product based on process data? which typically include a valid combination of measured material attributes and process controls. ICH Q8(R2).
- The control strategy can include the following? elements: procedural controls, in process controls, lot release testing, process monitoring, characterization testing, comparability testing and stability testing.

Life Cycle Management:

- In the QBD paradigm, process changes within} the design space will not require review or approval.
- Therefore, process improvements during the} product life cycle with regard to process consistency and throughput could take place with fewer post approval submissions.

Significance:

- Quality by Design means –designing and developing formulations and manufacturing processes to ensure a predefined quality.
- Quality by Design requires – understanding how} formulation and manufacturing process variables influence product quality.
- Quality by Design ensures – Product quality with effective control strategy

SIX SIGMA

- Six Sigma seeks to improve the quality of process outputs by identifying and removing the causes of defects. Six Sigma approach is a collection of managerial and statistical deficiencies in product. The concept of Variation states "NO two items will be perfectly identical.
- In a process that has achieved six sigma capability, the variation is small compared to the range of specification limit.
- A six-sigma process is one in which 99.9999966% of the products manufactured are statistically expected to be free of defects (3.4 defects per million).
- Six Sigma is a very clever way of branding and packaging many aspects of Total Quality Management (TQM). (TQM is a management approach to long–term success through customer satisfaction.)
- Manufacturing methods of six sigma are used in Batch production, Job production & Mass production.

The Characteristics of Six Sigma:

Statistical Quality Control: Six sigma is clearly derived from Greek letter sigma which is used to denote standard deviation in statistics which is used to measure nonconformance as far quality output is concerned.

Methodical Approach:The six sigma is not merely quality improvement strategy in the theory as it features a well-defined methodical approach of application in DMAIC and DMADV which can be used for quality production.

Fact and Data Based Approach: The statistical and methodical aspects of Six Sigma show the scientific basis of the technique. This accentuates an important aspect of Six Sigma that it is fact and data based

Project and Objective Based Focus: The Six Sigma process is implemented for an organization's project tailored to its specifications and requirement. The process is flexed to suit the requirements and conditions in which a project is operating to get the best results. Apart from that, the Six Sigma is also objective based. The management needs some incentive to invest in the Six Sigma process. It is aimed to enhance profitability and to generate financial.

The Customer Focus: The customer focus is fundamental to the Six Sigma approach. The quality improvement and control standards are based on the explicit customer requirements.

Teamwork Approach to Quality Management: The Six Sigma process requires organizations to get organized when it comes to controlling and improving quality. Six Sigma involves a lot of training depending on the role of an individual in the Quality Management team.

Six Sigma Objectives:

Overall Business Improvement: Six Sigma methodology focuses on business improvement. Beyond reducing the number of defects present in any given number of products.

Remedy Defects/Variability: Any business seeking improved numbers must reduce the number of defective products or services it produces. Defective products can harm customer satisfaction levels.

Reduce Costs: Reduced costs equal increased profits. A company implementing Six Sigma principles must look to reduce costs wherever it possibly can--without reducing quality.

Improve Cycle Time: Any reduction in the amount of time it takes to produce a product or perform a service means money saved, both in maintenance costs and personnel wages. Additionally, customer satisfaction improves when both retailers and end users receive products sooner than expected. The company that can get a product to its customer faster may win her business.

Increase Customer Satisfaction: Customer satisfaction depends upon successful resolution of all Six Sigma's other objectives. But customer satisfaction is an objective all its own.

Methodologies

Six Sigma projects follow two project methodologies:

1. DMAIC
2. DMADV

1. **DMAIC:** DMAIC is used for projects aimed at improving an existing business process. The DMAIC project methodology has Five phases:

    1. Define 2. Measure 3. Analyze 4. Improve 5. Control

    2. **DMADV:** DMADV is used for projects aimed at creating new product or process designs. DMADV project methodology has Five phase:

        1. Define 2. Measure 3. Analyze 4. Design 5. Verify

OUT OF SPECIFICATION (OOS)

Definition: The term OOS (out of specification), is defined as those results of in process or finished product testing, which falling out of specified limits, that are mentioned in compendia, drug master file, or drug application.

The OOS, may arise due to deviations in product manufacturing process, errors in testing procedure, or due to malfunctioning of analytical equipment.

The reasons for OOS can be classified as

1.Assignable

2. Non-Assignable.

CHANGE CONTROL

Definition:

Change control is a systematic approach to managing all changes made to a product or system. The purpose is to ensure that no unnecessary changes are made, that all changes are documented, that services are not unnecessarily disrupted and that resources are used efficiently.

Procedure:

1. The initiating department shall initiate the change as per the change control format
2. The initiating department shall furnish the details very clearly in the form for present process/use, proposed change, Justification & impact analysis and acceptance criteria.
3. The initiating department shall also define changes as major or minor based on product quality or its impact of safety, health, and environmental aspects. Some of the major and minor changes are listed below:

Major Changes: *For a substance of chemical and microbiological quality evaluation.*

- Addition or deletion of a step or addition of an alternative/new step in the formulation manufacturing process.
- Addition of a new manufacturing site with modification of the formulation manufacturing process described in the original dossier/ document.
- Change in input quantities of formulation manufacturing process.
- Changes in the quality of raw material(s) or key intermediate(s) used in the formulation manufacturing process.

Minor Changes:

- Change in the administrative references (name/company name, address) of the certificate holder.
- Change in the references (name/company name, address) of the manufacturing site.
- Change or updating of the methods of analysis used to test the substance.

- Change in the specifications of the substance.
- Change in supplier of starting and packing material.
- Change in the batch size.
- Addition of a new manufacturing site in the same site as described in the original dossier
- Change in the documents like SOPs etc.

Key Benefits of Change Control System:

- Structured and consistent approach towards managing change.
- Documenting the details of change.
- Routing of change requests to appropriate? individuals/team for approvals Documentation of change approvals and implementation.
- Maintenance of change history and easy retrieval of information.
- Tracking changes effectively and providing an audit trail.
- Demonstrate compliance to FDA regulations.

Quality Standard – ISO 9000

The ISO 9000 family of standards is related to quality management systems and designed to help organizations ensure that they meet the needs of customers and other stakeholders while meeting statutory and regulatory requirements.

ISO 9000 deals with the fundamentals of quality management systems, including the eight management principles on which the family of standards is based.

International standards promote international trade by providing one consistent set of requirements recognized around the world.

ISO 9000 can help a company satisfy its customers, meet regulatory requirements and achieve continual improvement. It provides the base level of a quality system, not a complete guarantee of quality.

Originally published in 1987 by the International Organization for Standardization (ISO), a specialized international agency for standardization composed of the national standards bodies of 90 countries.

Eight Quality Management Principles:

1. Customer focus
2. Leadership
3. Involvement of people Process approach
4. System approach to management
5. Continual improvement
6. Factual approach to decision making
7. Mutually beneficial supplier relationships

ISO 9000 Series:

Advantages

ISO 9000: • Explains fundamental quality concepts and provides guidelines for the selection and application of each standard.

ISO 9001: • Model for quality assurance in design, development, production, installation, and servicing.

ISO 9002: Model for quality assurance in the production and installation of manufacturing systems.

ISO 9003: Quality assurance in final inspection and testing.

ISO 9004: Guidelines for the applications of standards in quality management and quality systems

- Quality is maintained,
- ISO registration also has a significant bearingon market credibility as well.
- Opportunity to compete with larger companies.
- More time spent on customer focus.
- Confirmation that your company is committed to quality.
- May facilitate trade and increased market opportunities.
- Can increase customer confidence and satisfaction.

INTERNATIONAL ORGANIZATION FOR STANDARDIZATION (ISO 14000)

- ISO is an international standard-setting body? composed of representatives from various national standards organizations.
- Founded on 23 February 1947, the organization? promotes worldwide proprietary, industrial and commercial standards. It is headquartered in Geneva, Switzerland.
- ISO 14000 is a family of standards related to environmental management that exists to help organizations.
- Minimize how their operations (processes etc.) negatively affect the environment (i.e. cause adverse changes to air, water, or land)
- Comply with applicable laws, regulations, and other environmentally oriented requirements continually improve in the above.

ENVIRONMENTAL MANAGEMENT SYSTEM:

An Environmental Management System (EMS) is a framework that helps a company achieve its environmental goals through consistent control of its operations. The assumption is that this increased control will improve the environmental performance of the company.

STANDARDS UNDER ISO 14000 SERIES:

- ISO 14001 is an EMS standard.
- ISO 14010 series of standards are about auditing.?
- ISO 14020 is about environmental labeling.?
- ISO 14030 is a standard on environmental? performance evaluation.
- ISO 14040 series are on environmental life cycle?assessment(LAC)

ISO 14001 STANDARD:

ISO 14001 is known as a generic management system standard, meaning that it is relevant to any organization seeking to improve and manage resources more effectively. This includes:

- Single site to large multi-national companies.
- High risk companies to low risk service organizations.
- Manufacturing, process and the service industries; including local governments.
- All industry sectors including public and private sectors.
- Original equipment manufacturers and their suppliers.

BASIC PRINCIPLES AND METHODOLOGY:

  - Plan
  - Do
  - Check
  - Act

BENEFITS:

- It can be applied to any type of organization.
- It helps in maintaining an efficient quality system in an organization.
- It creates confidence in customer on the quality of? product supplied.
- It acts as competitive barrier.

National Accreditation Board for Testing and Calibration Laboratories (NABL)

NABL specifies the general requirements for the competence to carry out tests and calibrations, including sampling. It covers testing and calibration performed using standard methods, non- standard methods, and laboratory-developed methods.

NABL is an autonomous society providing Accreditation (Recognition) of Technical competence of a testing, calibration, medical laboratory & Proficiency testing provider (PTP) & Reference Material Producer (RMP).

NABL stands for National Accreditation Board for Testing And Calibration Laboratories. NABL has agreements with ILAC (International Laboratory Accreditation Conference) and APLAC (Asia Pacific Laboratory Accreditation Cooperation). These are especially valuable for International recognition and mutual acceptance of test results. In short accreditation has worldwide acceptance.

NABL Mission:

To strengthen the accreditation system accepted across the globe by providing high quality, value driven services, fostering APLAC/ILAC MRA, empanelling competent assessors, creating awareness among the stake holders, initiating new programs supporting accreditation activities and pursuing organisational excellence.

Benefits of Accreditation:

1. Potential increase in business due to enhanced customer confidence and satisfaction. Savings in terms of time and money due to reduction or elimination of the need for re-testing .
2. Better control of laboratory operations and feedback to laboratories? as to whether they have sound Quality Assurance System and are technically competent.
3. Increase of confidence in Testing / Calibration data and personnel performing work.
4. Customers can search and identify the laboratories accredited by NABL for their specific requirements from the directory of Accredited Laboratories.
5. Users of accredited laboratories will enjoy greater access for their products, in both domestic and international markets, when tested by accredited laboratories.
6. Proficiency testing providers play an important role in the value chain for assurance of products and services. Being an accredited PTP gives the organization credibility for their PT services. The benefits of proficiency testing are widely recognized. These include

- Comparison of a facility's performance with that of other participating (peer) facilities.
- Monitoring of a long-term facility performance.
- Improvement in the performance of tests/calibrations following investigation and identification of the cause(s) of unsatisfactory PT performance, and the introduction of corrective action to prevent re-occurrence.
- Evaluation of methods, including the establishment of method precision and accuracy.
- Confidence building with interested parties, e.g. customers, accreditation bodies, regulators.

NABL Accreditation is currently given in the following fields and disciplines:

- Biological
- Chemical·
- Electrical
- Electronics
- Fluid-Flow
- Mechanical
- Non-Destructive Testing
- Radiological
- Thermal
- Forensic

GOOD LABORATORY PRACTICES (GLP)

Definition: GLP embodies a set of principles that provides a framework within which laboratory studies are planned performed, monitored, and archived and reported.

Purpose of GLPs:

1. GLP is to certify that every step of the analysis is valid or Not.

2. Assure the quality & integrity of data submitted to FDA in support of the safety of regulated products.
3. GLPs have heavy emphasis on data recording, record & specimen retention.

GOOD LABORATORY PRACTICES PRINCIPLES.

1. Test Facility Organisation and Personnel.
2. Quality Assurance Programme(QAP).
3. Facilities.
4. Apparatus, Material and Reagents.
5. Test systems.
6. Test and Reference Substances.
7. Standard Operating Procedures(SOP).
8. Performance of The Study.
9. Reporting of Study Results.
10. Storage and Retention of Records and materials.

Benefits of good laboratory practices:

1. It will give better image of company as a Quality producer in Global market.
2. Provide hot tips on analysis of data as well as measure uncertainty and perfect record keeping.
3. Provide guidelines for doing testing and measurement in detail.
4. Provide guidelines and better control for maintenance of instruments, environment control, preservation of test records etc.

CHAPTER V

INDIAN REGULATORY REQUIREMENTS

Central Drugs Standard Control Organization (CDSCO) and state licensing authority: Organization and Responsibilities, Certificate of Pharmaceutical Product (COPP), Regulatory requirements and approval procedures of New drugs.

Introduction-

The drug regulatory authority (DRA) is the agency that develops and implements most of the legislation and regulations on pharmaceuticals. Its main task is to ensure the quality, safety and efficacy of drugs, and the accuracy of product information. This is done by making certain rules that the manufacture, procurement, import, export, distribution, supply and sale of drugs, product promotion and advertising, and clinical trials are carried out according to specified standards.

Functions of Regulatory Authority:

- Product registration (drug evaluation and authorization, and monitoring of drug efficacy and safety.
- Regulation of drug manufacturing, importation, and distribution.
- Regulation & Control of drug promotion and information.
- Adverse drug reaction (ADR) monitoring.
- Licensing of premises, persons and practices.
- Main goal of drug regulation is to guarantee the safety, efficacy and quality of drugs.

Central Drugs Standard Control Organization (CDSCO)-

Central Drugs Standard Control Organization (CDSCO) exercises regulatory control over the quality of drugs, cosmetics and notified medical devices in the country. The CDSCO of India is main regulatory body for regulation of pharmaceutical, medical devices and Clinical Trials.

It is the Central Drug Authority for discharging functions assigned to the Central Government under the Drugs and Cosmetics Act. Its Head quarter is located at FDA Bhawan, Kotla Road, New Delhi and functions under the Directorate General of Health Services, ministry of health and family welfare Government of India.

It is divided into zonal offices which do pre-licensing and post-licensing inspections, post- market surveillance, and recalls when needed.

Vision: To Protect & Promote Health in India

Mission: To safeguard and enhance the public health by assuring the safety, efficacy and quality of drugs, cosmetics and medical devices.

Drugs Controller General of India (DCGI)

- He/she is a responsible for approval of New Drugs, Medical devices and Clinical Trails to be conducted in India.
- He is appointed by the central government under the DCGI the State drug control organization will be functioning.
- The DCGI is advised by the Drug Technical Advisory Board (DTAB) and the Drug Consultative Committee (DCC).

The DCGI is responsible for handling matters of product approval and approval standards, clinical trials, introduction of new drugs, and import licenses for new drugs. A drug may be licensed for manufacturing in a state only once it has been approved by CDSCO.

Process of drug regulation

The DC Act entrusts CDSCO with the responsibility for the approval of new drugs, and the conduct of clinical trials in the country, as well as laying down the standards for drugs, controlling the quality of imported drugs, oversight over the SDRAs, and an advisory role in ensuring uniformity in the enforcement of the DC Act itself.

CDSCO approves new drugs based on a combination of non-clinical data, clinical trial data (focusing on safety and efficacy) from abroad as well as in India, and the regulatory status of the drug in other countries. The law around new drug approvals is contained in Rules 122 A, 122 B, 122D, 122 DA, 122 DAA, 122 DAB, 122 DAC, 122 DB, 122 DD and 122 E of

Schedule-Y of the DC Rules. The law permits a waiver of requiring local clinical trials if the Licensing Authority decides it is in the public interest to grant permission to import / manufacture the new drug on the basis of data available from other countries. In special circumstances, such as drugs required in life threatening / serious diseases or diseases of special relevance to the Indian health scenario, the law permits the Licensing Authority to abbreviate, defer or omit clinical data requirements altogether.

Applications for approval of New Drugs are evaluated by the 12 Subject Expert Committee (SEC) (formerly referred to as New Drug Advisory Committees (NDAC), consisting of experts usually drawn from Government Medical Colleges and Institutes across India. The approval or otherwise is granted based on the recommendations of these committees. Overall, this has put considerable cloud over the new drugs approval and regulatory process in India, and with the ban being issued by the government rather than by CDSCO, this particularly casts a shadow on the legitimacy of CDSCO as a regulatory body.

Besides approval, the other important regulatory roles are regarding licensing and inspections. Sections 22 and 23 of the DC Act give the Drug Inspectors (DI) the power to inspect premises manufacturing or selling drugs or cosmetics and take samples of any drug or cosmetic in exchange of its fair price and a written acknowledgement. Where the sample has been taken for testing or analysis, the DI must inform about its purpose in writing to the owner of the premises. The provisions also direct the DI to divide the samples into four (three, if taken from the manufacturer) properly sealed portions or take as many units of the drug. The Government Analyst under Section 25 of the DC Act must then prepare a signed report which is then taken to be a conclusive fact upon the standard of quality of the drug. These provisions are complemented by the DC Rules which elaborate on the duties of the Government Analyst, the Drug Inspector and the Licensing Authority.

In 2017, the DC Rules were amended, making it mandatory that before the grant of manufacturing license, the manufacturing establishment is to be inspected jointly by the Drug Inspectors of both the central government and the concerned state government. The amendment also made a similar joint inspection mandatory for manufacturing premises for not less that once every three years or as needed per the risk-based approach. Recently, the DTAB has recommended amending the DC Act to authorize Licensing Authorities to issue stop-sale orders for drug retailers. Earlier, this power to issue stop-sale orders was available to the Licensing Authorities in cases of manufacturing non-compliances only.

Organization of CDSCO

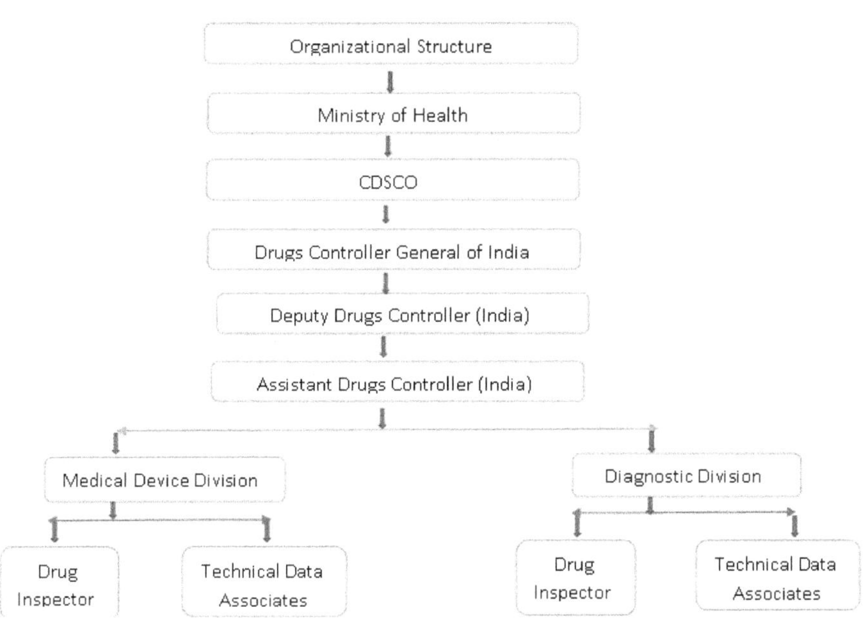

Fig 5.1 : Organization of CDSCO

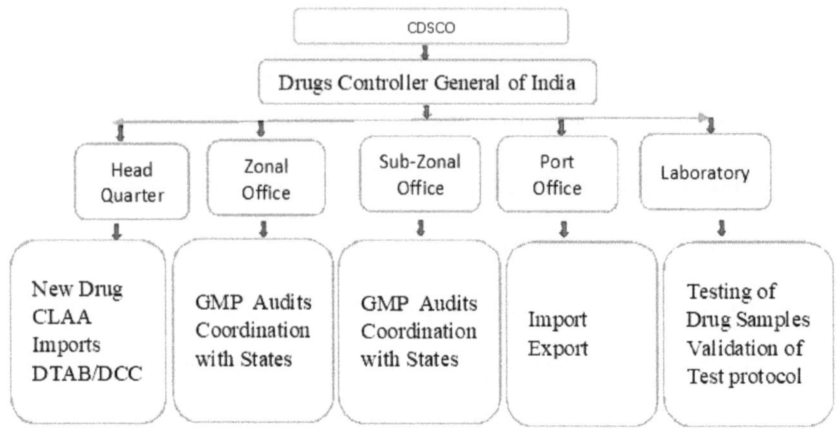

Enter Caption

Zonal offices

- Mumbai
- Kolkata
- Chennai
- Ghaziabad
- Ahemdabad
- Hyderabad

The zonal offices work in close collaboration with the State Dug Control Administration and assist them in securing uniform enforcement of the drug act and other connected leistations, on all India basis. These are involved in GMP audits and inspection of manufacturing units of large volume parental, sera, vaccine and blood products.

Sub-zonal office:

I. Chandigarh
II. Jammu
III. Bangalore

These centre co-ordinate with state drug control authorities under their jurisdiction for uniform standard of inspection and enforcement.

Functions of Port Offices of CDSCO

- Scrutiny of bills of entry with a view to ensuring that imported drugs comply with the regulations. •To check the shipping bills for export for statistical data and keep control under the regulations
- To ensure that no New Drug is imported into the country unless its import is permitted by the Drugs Licensing Authority under Rules 122 A & 30-AA.
- To ensure that small quantities of drugs imported for clinical trials or for personal use are duly permitted under Test License (11 or 11-A) or Permit License as (12 B) as the case may be.
- Maintenance of Statistics regarding import and export of drugs and cosmetics.
- Coordination with Customs authorities.
- Coordination with States Drugs Controllers and Zonal Offices for post-import checks.
- Preparation of monthly / quarterly / annual reports.
- To draw samples from import/export and re-import consignments.

Central Drugs Testing Laboratories (CDTL)

- Central Drug Laboratory, Kolkata
- Central Drug Testing Laboratory, Mumbai
- Central Drug Testing Laboratory, Chennai
- Central Drug Laboratory, Kasauli
- Regional Drug Testing Laboratory, Guwahati
- Regional Drug Testing Laboratory, Chandigarh

These laboratories are established under the Indian Drug and Cosmetic Act, 1940 and responsible for quality control of drugs and cosmetics in the country.

The functions of this laboratories include:

1. Statutory functions:

a. Analytical quality control of majority of the imported drug available in Indian market.
b. Acting as an Appellate authority in matters of disputes relating to quality of Drugs.
c. Laying down standards of drugs, cosmetics, diagnostics and devices.
d. Laying down regulatory measures, amendments to Acts and Rules.
e. To regulate market authorisation of new drugs.
f. To regulate clinical research in India.
g. To approve licenses to manufacture certain categories of drugs as Central Licence approving Authority i.e. for Blood Banks, Large Volume Parenteral and Vaccines & Sera.
h. To regulate the standards of imported drugs.
a. Work relating to the Drugs Technical Advisory Board (DTAB) and Drugs Consultative Committee (DCC).
j. Testing of drugs by Central Drugs Labs
k. Publication of Indian Pharmacopoeia.

2. Other functions:

l. Collection, storage and distribution of International Standard reference preparations of Drug & Pharmaceutical substances.
m. Training of Drug Analysts deputed by State Drug Control Laboratories and other Institutions.
n. To advise the Central Drug Control Administration in respect of quality & toxicity of drug awaiting licence.
o. To work out analytical specifications for preparation of Monographs for the Indian Pharmacopeia & the Homeopathic Pharmacopeia of India.
p. Monitoring in the WHO GMP certification scheme.
q. Screening of drug formulations available in Indian market.
r. Evaluation /screening of applications for granting NOC for export of unapproved /banned drugs.

Functions of CDSCO in Centre

- Approval of new drugs and clinical trials.
- Import Registration and Licensing
- Licensing of Blood Banks, LVPs, Vaccines, r-DNA products and some Medical devices and Diagnostic agents.
- Amendment to D&C Act and Rules.
- Participation in WHO GMP certification schemes.
- Banning of drugs and cosmetics.
- Grant to test license, personal license, NOC's for export.
- Testing of drugs by Central Labs.
- Publication of Indian Pharmacopoeia.
- Monitoring adverse drug reactions.
- Guidance on Technical matters.

Responsibilities of Central Authority

CDSCO: For implementing and to revise the same as notified, from time to time by the authority.

- Initiate in framing of rules, regulations and guidance documents to match the contemporary issues in compliance with the requirements of Drugs & Cosmetics Act 1940 and Rules 1945.
- Facilitate in Uniform implementation of the provisions of the Drugs & Cosmetics Act 1940 and Rules 1945.
- Function as Central license Approving Authority under the provisions of Drugs and Cosmetics Act 1940 and Rules 1945.
- Collaboration with other similar International agencies. • Providing training to the Indian regulatory personnel.
- Approval of New Drugs
- Clinical Trials in the country
- Laying down the standards for Drugs
- Control over the quality of imported Drugs
- Coordination of the activities of State Drug CO
- Providing expert advice with a view of bringing about the uniformity in the enforcement of the Drugs and Cosmetics Act

Drug Technical Advisory Board (DTAB)

Ex-Officio:

1. Director General of Health Services (Chairman)
2. Drugs Controller, India
3. Director of the Central Drugs Laboratory, Calcutta
4. Director of the Central Research Institute, Kasauli
5. President of Medical Council of India
6. President of the Pharmacy Council of India
7. Director of Central Drug Research Institute, Lucknow

Nominated:

1. Two persons by the Central Government.
2. One person by the Central Government from the pharmaceutical industry
3. Two persons holding the appointment of Government Analyst under this Act,

Elected:

1. One person, to be elected by the Executive Committee of the Pharmacy Council of India,
2. One person, to be elected by the Executive Committee of the Medical Council of India,
3. One pharmacologist to be elected by the Governing Body of the Indian Council of Medical Research;
4. One person to be elected by the Central Council of the Indian Medical Association;
5. One person to be elected by the Council of the Indian Pharmaceutical Association

Function:

To advise the Central Government and the State Governments on technical matters. To carry out the other functions assigned to it by this Act.

The Drugs Consultative Committee (DCC)

- It is also an advisory body constituted by central government. Constitution:
- Two representatives of the Central Government
- One representative of each State Government

Functions:

- To advise the Central Government, the State Governments and the Drugs Technical Advisory Board on any other matter tending to secure uniformity throughout India in the administration of this Act.
- There is separate "The Ayurvedic, Siddha, & Unani Drugs Consultative Committee constituted under sec 33 D of the Act.

State Drug Regulatory Authorities (SDRAs) :

It was established under the DC Act are responsible for licensing of manufacturing establishments and sale premises, undertaking inspections of such premises to ensure compliance with license conditions, drawing samples for testing and monitoring of quality of drugs, taking actions like suspension/cancellation of licenses, surveillance over sale of spurious and adulterated drugs, instituting legal prosecution when required, and monitoring of objectionable advertisements for drugs.

The State Drug Controller (SDC) heads the SDRA and reports to a joint secretary in the health department of the state government. A typical SDRA has Drug Inspectors reporting to the Deputy Drugs Controller who also acts as the Licensing Authority for the state. Administrative matters such as departmental budgeting, appointments, training of officers, and allotment of funds and resources for inspections, falls under the jurisdiction of the state governments. This report found that a number of SDRAs were conjoined with the food regulatory departments (FDAs) of the state, making it difficult to clearly demarcate the available funds and resources between the two.

Function of State Licensing Authorities

1. Licensing of drug manufacturing and sales establishments
2. Licensing of drug testing laboratories.
3. Approval of drug formulations for manufacture.
4. Monitoring of quality of Drugs & Cosmetics, manufactured by respective state units and those marketed in the state.
5. Investigation and prosecution in respect of contravention of legal provisions.
6. Administrative actions.
7. Pre- and post- licensing inspection
8. Recall of sub-standard drugs.

Responsibilities of State Authority

- Manufacturing, sales, distribution of Drugs licensing drug testing laboratories.
- Approving drug formulations for manufacture
- Carrying out pre- and post-licensing inspections
- Overseeing the manufacturing process for drugs manufactured by respective state units and those marketed in the state

Certificate of Pharmaceutical Product (COPP) Definition-

The WHO Certification Scheme for a Certificate of Pharmaceutical Product (COPP) is an international voluntary agreement to provide assurance to countries participating in the Scheme, about the quality of pharmaceutical products moving in international commerce.

Certificate of pharmaceutical product is a scheme developed by the WHO in response to the request of WHO Member States to facilitate international trade in pharmaceutical products between Member States. It was first developed in 1975. Since then it has been revised in 1988, 1992and in 1997.

Purpose-

A COPP is in the format recommended by the WHO. It is the importing country who requires the COPP for the pharmaceutical product and a special type of certificate which enables a given pharmaceutical product to be registered and marketed in the exporting country of interest and forms parts of the marketing authorization application.

This certificate describes the characteristics of the medicinal product approved in the exporting country, includes information about the applicant of the certificate and is according with the model recommended by the World Health Organization. This is a certificate issued by the Inspectorate establishing the status of the pharmaceutical, biological, radiopharmaceutical or veterinary product listed and the GMP status of the fabricator of the product.

Ideally, a COPP should not be required in countries that have the capabilities to conduct full reviews. The COPP should be used when a pharmaceutical product is under consideration for a product licence/ marketing authorisation or when administrative action is required to renew, extend or vary such a licence.

Aim and Scope-

The COPP is the legal document that declares a certain manufacturing company is legally allowed to sell their pharmaceutical product in the country they are producing. When registering a pharmaceutical product overseas, the Government body in charge of approving the application will usually require a COPP to ensure that the product is being sold as a commercial finished product in the country that is producing it.

A COPP demonstrates in question that the imported medicine is of the appropriate standard of quality, safety and efficacy to allow marketing in their market, having undergone rigorous testing and examination to Regulatory Authorities in the exporting country and also demonstrates that it follows the correct guidelines and procedures of Good Manufacturing Practice (GMP), increasing the level of quality and indeed safety of the product. The COPP is needed when the product tends that it is intended for registration or its renewal (licensing, authorization or prolongation)) by the importing country, with the scope that the product is distributed or commercialized in that country.

Certification has been recommended by WHO to help undersized drug regulatory authorities or drug regulatory authorities without proper quality assurance facilities in importing countries to assess the quality of pharmaceutical products as prerequisite of registration or importation.

Need & Importance of COPP:

To obtain global marketing approval for any pharmaceutical product (whether intended for animal/human use) one of the key documents required is a COPP, which has been recommended by the WHO. A COPP is issued by the authorized body of the exporting country and is intended for use by the competent authority within an importing country: when a pharmaceutical product is under consideration for a product license/ marketing authorization that will authorize its importation and sale in the importing country; when administrative action is required to renew, extend vary or review such license.

A COPP is issued for human drugs (pharmaceutical, biological and radiopharmaceutical) as well as for veterinary drugs (food producing animals and non-food producing animals). For each medicinal product (Trade Name / Pharmaceutical Form / Strength) is issued a certificate stating the country to export. These Certificates are issued to the marketing authorizations holders (MAH) for medicinal products (with valid Marketing Authorization) or their representatives, manufacturers (without Marketing Authorization and with manufacturing authorization valid) or wholesale distributor authorized by the MAH to consult the information for the medicinal product(s)

Types of COPP:

1.

WHO 1975 type COPP-

The WHO 1975 version is a certificate to be issued by exporting country regulatory authority stating: a) the authorized product has to be placed on the market for its use in the country also,

the permit number and issue date, or b) that the nonauthorized product has placed on the market for its use in the country and also add the reasons why it is needed; Also, that; a) As recommended by World Health Organization, the manufacturer of product conforms to GMP requirements. b) only within the country of origin the products to be sold or distributed; or c) To be exported to manufacturing plant where the product is produced and at suitable intervals subject to inspections.

2.

WHO 1988 type COPP-

Unlike the WHO 1975 version, the competent authority of the exporting country should have: all labelling copies and product detailed information in the country of origin.

3.

WHO 1992 type COPP-

This is intended for use by the competent authority of an importing country in two situations:

a. When the question arises related to importation and sale license; and b) For license renew, extend, review or changes.

The following information required for the certificate:

i. Whether a licensed product is required to be placed on the market or not.
ii. Also if the satisfied information submitted by the applicant that the certifying authority of the manufacture of the product undertaken by another party
iii. iii) Inspection have been carried out of the manufacturer of product;
iv. If the certificate is provisional or permanent;
v. Is the dosage forms, packages and/or labels of a finished dosage form manufactured by an independent company or by the applicant;
vi. states the names of the importing and exporting (certifying) countries

Here besides three types of COPPs also we have another specific type of the U.S. FDA COPPs. The U.S. FDA issued "Pilot- COPP" for the remaining products which are neither exported nor manufactured in the United States. It is only when no other country has given an approval for the finished medicinal product registration.

Content of the COPP

A CPP has two distinct parts: a) Evidence of quality, safety, and efficacy (QSE) Review and

b. Evidence of Compliance with GMP.

Content and format

- Importing country:
- Exporting country:
- Name, form of dosage and its composition of the product (API per unit dose).
- Registration Information (licensing)

- Marketing status of the product in the exporting country.
- license no. of product (containing license holder details; involvement of license holder in manufacturing if any) and also add date of issue,
- Summary of technical basis on which the product has been licensed (if required by the issuing authority)
- Currently marketed product's information
- Details about the product's applicant
- If lacking is there in the exporting country, need to mention the information about reasons.

Key challenges of the interpretation of the COPP scheme

- Difference in product names between certifying and requesting countries.
- The COPP confirms GMP status, additional GMP certificates should not be necessary.
- The COPP is a legal document, additional apostille and/or legalization should not be requested.
- Requirements for the 'country of origin' or 'source country' have multiple definitions and should be clarified as it could refer to the country of any one of the following: first approval or marketing, manufacture, packaging, final release, or main headquarters of the pharmaceutical company.
- The COPP provides evidence of a positive QSE review in the issuing country. A full dossier should not be requested.
- The scheme refers only to the manufacturer of the dosage form but some importing countries require additional manufacturers to be listed.
- The COPP issued is a snapshot of the Market Authorization (MA) in the issuing country and may not necessarily reflect the entire situation in the importing country.

Advantages of the scheme

- To grow business in foreign country, necessary to obtain the COPP certificates by pharmaceutical companies.
- The Scheme provides the standard format that is expected to be used. Enables recipient COPP countries to gain assurance on the QSE of the product in the issuing country.
- Obliges certifying authorities to disclose important information to the importing country.
- By supporting the review and approval process it facilitates patient access to quality medicines.

The COPP may be required to support a regulatory submission. This can be submitted at the beginning of, or during the health authority review. According to the WHO Scheme, COPPs should not be required in countries that require full ICH CTD dossiers and have the capability to conduct full QSE reviews.

The COPP only reflects the approved manufacturing sourcing route of the certifying country.

Most recipient authorities expect that the drug product they will receive mirrors that which has been approved by the authority issuing the COPP. When developing a global submission strategy COPP requirements are considered early during the planning phase. If required HAs should be open to discussion in advance of the regulatory submission to give advice and agree on the content of the submission including the COPP to move forward as quickly possible.

Certificate of a pharmaceutical product

This certificate, which is in the format recommended by WHO, establishes the status of the pharmaceutical product and of the applicant for the certificate in the exporting country. It is for a single product only since manufacturing arrangements and approved information for different dosage forms and different strengths can vary.

The COPP provides the information of the following:

1. **Certificate number of COPP**: The certificate number of COPP should be enclosed in the specified format recommended by WHO.
2. **Name of exporting country i.e. (certifying country):** The name of the country (certified country) to which the product is being exported must

be mentioned in the certificate.

3. **Name of importing country i.e. (requesting country):** The name of the countries (requesting countries) from which the product is being imported from certified country must be mentioned in the certificate.
4. Name and dosage form of the product.

Active ingredient	International Non-proprietary Names (INNs) or national non-proprietary names
Amount per unit dose	The formula (complete composition) of the dosage form should be given on the certificate or be appended.
Complete composition including excipients	Details of quantitative composition are preferred but their provision is subject to the agreement of the product-license holder.
Is this product licensed to be placed on the market for use in the exporting country?(yes/no)	When applicable, append details of any restriction applied to the sale, distribution or administration of the product that is specified in the product license.

Table No.5.1: Essentials of Product

5. Status of the product actually on the market in the exporting country:

If the product is actually marketed in the exporting country, the COPP should be provided with the following details:

- Number of product license and date of issue: Indicate, when applicable, if the license is provisional, or the product has not yet been approved.
- Product license holder (name and address):
- Status of product license holder:

Specify whether the person responsible for placing the product on the market:

a. manufactures the dosage form;

b. packages and/or labels a dosage form manufactured by an independent company; or
c. is involved in none of the above.

- **For categories b and c** the name and address of the manufacturer producing the dosage form is This information can only be provided with the consent of the product-license holder or, in the case of non-registered products, the applicant. Non-completion of this section indicates that the party concerned has not agreed to inclusion of this information. It should be noted that information concerning the site of production is part of the product license. If the production site is changed, the license has to be updated or it is no longer valid.
- Is a summary basis for approval appended? (yes/no)

This refers to the document, prepared by some national regulatory authorities, that summarizes the technical basis on which the product has been licensed.

- Is the attached, officially approved product information complete and consonent with the license? (yes/no/not provided)

This refers to product information approved by the competent national regulatory authority, such as Summary Product Characteristics (SPC).

- Applicant for certificate, if different from license holder (name and address)

In this circumstance, permission for issuing the certificate is required from the product-license holder. This permission has to be provided to the authority by the applicant.

6. Periodic inspection of the manufacturing plant by the certifying authority:

If the certifying authority arrange for periodic inspection of the manufacturing plant in which the dosage form is produced, the following details were to be included in the COPP.

- Periodicity of routine inspections (years):

- Has the manufacture of this type of dosage form been inspected? (yes/no)
- Do the facilities and operations conform to GMP as recommended by the World Health Organization? (yes/no/not applicable)

7. The information submitted by the applicant satisfy the certifying authority on all aspects of the manufacture of the product undertaken by another party:

This section is to be completed when the product-license holder or applicant conforms to status

b. or (c) as described in note above. It is of particular importance when foreign contractors are involved in the manufacture of the product. In these circumstances the applicant should supply the certifying authority with information to identify the contracting parties responsible for each stage of manufacture of the finished dosage form, and the extent and nature of any controls exercised over each of these parties.

8. Other details of Manufacturing premises:

The following details which is to be enclosed in the COPP are,

- Address of certifying authority
- Telephone and Fax
- Name of authorized person
- Signature
- Stamp and date

How to obtain COPP?

- To obtain a COPP, a request is made to the exporting country's health authority by the Marketing Authorization Holder (MAH).
- An authorized person issues the COPP and returns it to the MAH. Also other documents required to obtain a COPP including an application for Export Certificate form, evidence of a GMP certificate (if applicable), Manufacturing License and the last approved SPC (Summary of Product Characteristics).

Types of drugs for which COPPs may be issued

- Approved drug products
- Active pharmaceutical ingredients (API)
- Over the counter drug (OTC) products
- Unapproved drug products
- Homeopathic drugs

Who can apply for COPP?

- A complete application for export certification must be submitted by the person/company who exports the drug.
- The certification is intended for a drug which : meets the applicable requirements of the Act or Food Drug and Cosmetic Act 801(e)(1) requirements [21 U.S.C.381(e)(1)]

Process to apply for a COPP

a. Submit Form no. 3613b– Located on the FDA internet www.fda.gov/downloads/AboutFDA/Reports Manuals Forms/Forms/UCM052388
b. Requirements for COPP application:

- Applicant Contact Information
- Trade name (the drug product's brand name)
- Bulk Substance Generic Name
- Name of Applicant
- Status of Product License holder
- Listing of manufacturing location on COPP
- Complete Manufacturing Facility Address
- Facility Registration Number
- Importing countries
- Authorization to Release Information

- Number of certificates requested
- Certification Statement
- Billing contact
- Marketing Status in the Exporting Country

Process Time of COPP:

- Drugs in compliance are normally issued within twenty (20) government working days of receipt of complete and an accurate COPP application.

Certificates may not be issued

- Returned – missing information application with a letter identifying the missing information.
- Rejected – manufacturing facilities are not in compliance with good manufacturing practices (GMPs).
- Denied – drug products are not compliance as per regulation (e.g., misbranded drug)

Expiration of COPP

- Certificate expires on 2 years from the notarization date or as noted. ? After expiry date, a new COPP application has to be submitted.

Format of Certificate of Pharmaceutical Products (COPP) (as per WHO GMP guidelines)

No. of Certificate:

Exporting (certifying) country:

Importing (requesting) country:

Name and dosage form of product:

Active ingredient(s) and amount(s) per unit dose: -------------------------

1. Is this product Licensed to be placed on the market for use in the exporting country? If Yes, complete Box A. If No complete Box B.

A.

Product -license Holder (name and address): -

Status of license Holder- a/b/c (key in appropriate category)

Number of product License and date of issue: ----------------------------

Is an approved technical summary appended? Yes/ No

Is the attached, officially approved product information complete and consonant with the License? Yes/no/not provided (key in as appropriate)

Applicant for certificate, if different from License holder (name and address): ------------------

B.

Applicant for certificate (name and address): ---

Status of applicant: a/b/c (key in appropriate category) Why is marketing authorization lacking?

Not required/not requested/under consideration/refused (key is as appropriate) Remark:

2. Does the certifying authority arrange for periodic inspection of the manufacturing plant in which the dosage form is produced? Yes/no/not applicable (key in as appropriate)

If no or not applicable proceed to question 3.

2.1 Periodicity of routine inspections (years): ____________________

2.2 Has the manufacture of this type of dosage form been inspected? Yes/no (key in as appropriate)

2.3 Do the facilities and operations conform to GMP as recommended by the World Health Organization? 15 Yes/no (key in as appropriate)

3. Does the information submitted by the applicant satisfy the certifying authority on all aspects of the manufacture of the product? Yes/no (key in as appropriate)

If no, explain:

Address of certifying authority:

Telephone number:Fax number:

Name of authorized person:

Signature:

Stamp and date:

Approval of New Drug in India

If any company in India wants to manufacture or import a new drug, they need to apply to seek permission from the licensing authority (DCGI) by filing in Form 44 also submitting the data

as given in Schedule Y of Drugs and Cosmetics Act 1940 and Rules 1945.To prove its efficacy and safety in Indian population they need to conduct clinical trials in accordance with the guidelines specified in Schedule Y and submit the report of such clinical trials in specified format.

Demonstration of safety and efficacy of the drug product for use in humans is essential before the drug product can be approved for import or manufacturing of new drug by the applicant by Central Drugs Standard Control Organization (CDSCO). The regulations under Drugs and Cosmetics Act 1940 and its rules 1945, 122A, 122B and 122D describe the information required for approval of an application to import or manufacture of new drug for marketing. For an investigational new drug, the sponsor needs to provide detailed information to the DCGI about:

1. Generic name
2. Patent status
3. Brief description of physico-chemical/biological
4. Technical information like

    a. Stability b) Specifications c) Manufacturing process d) Worldwide regulatory status e) Animal pharmacology and toxicity studies

5. Published clinical trial reports
6. Proposed protocol and pro forma
7. Trial duration
8. During master file
9. Undertaking to Report Serious or Life-threatening Adverse Drug Reactions.

The information regarding the prescription, samples and testing protocols, product monographs, labels must also be submitted. It usually takes 3 months for clinical trial approval in India. The clinical trials can be registered in the Clinical Trials Registry of India (CTRI) giving details of the clinical trials and the subjects involved in the trials. The rules to be followed under The Drugs and Cosmetics Rules 1945 are:

1. Rule 122 A -: Application for permission to import new drug
2. Rule 122 B- Application for approval to manufacture new drug other than the drugs specified under Schedule C and C (1).
3. Rule 22 D- P Application for permission to import or manufacture fixed dose combination.
4. Rule 122 DA- Application for permission to conduct clinical trials for New Drug/Investigational New Drug
5. Rule 122 E - Definition of New Drugs*

There's a provision in Rule-122A of Drug and Cosmetic Act 1940 and Rules 1945, that if the licensing authority finds out that if everything is in the interest of public health then he may allow the import of new drugs, based on the data of the trials done in other countries. Another provision is Rule-122A is that clinical trial may be allowed in any new drug case, which are approved and already being used for many years in other countries.

Similarly, in Rule 122-B, application for approval to manufacture New Drug other than the drugs classifiable under Schedules C and C (1) and Permission to import or manufacture fixed dose combination (122-D).

Purpose-

The main purpose of regulating all the medicinal products by regulatory agencies is to safeguard public health. Regulatory agencies work is to make sure that the pharmaceutical companies comply with al, the regulations and standards, so that the patient's well-being is protected.

Through the International Conference on Harmonization (ICH) process, the Common Technical Document (CTD) guidance has been developed for Japan, European Union, and United States.

Most countries have adopted the CTD format. Hence, CDSCO has also decided to adopt CTD format for technical requirements for registration of pharmaceutical products for human use.

It is apparent that this structured application with comprehensive and rational contents will help the CDSCO to review and take necessary actions in a better way and would also ease the preparation of electronic submissions, which may happen in the near future at CDSCO.

New Drug Application (NDA)

New Drug Application (NDA) is an application submitted to the individual regulatory authority for authorization to market a new drug i.e. innovative product. To gain this permission a sponsor submits preclinical and clinical test data for analyzing the drug information, description of manufacturing procedures.

After NDA received by the agency, it undergoes a technical screening. This evaluation ensures that sufficient data and information have been submitted in each area to justify "filing" the application that is FDA formal review.

At the conclusion of FDA review of an NDA, there are 3 possible actions that can send to sponsor:

- Not approvable- in this letter list of deficiencies and explain the reason.
- Approvable - it means that the drug can be approved but minor deficiencies that can be corrected like-labelling changes and possible request commitment to do post-approval studies.
- Approval- it state that the drug is approved.

If the action taken is either an approvable or a not approvable, then FDA provides applicant with an opportunity to meet with agency and discuss the deficiencies.

Different Phases of clinical trials:

- Pre- clinical study - Mice, Rat, Rabbit, Monkeys
- Phase I - Human pharmacology trial - estimation of safety and tolerability
- Phase II - Exploratory trial - estimation of effectiveness and short-term side effects
- Phase III - Confirmatory trial - Confirmation of therapeutic benefits
- Phase IV Post marketing trial - Studies done after drug approval

Some of the rules & guidelines that should be followed for regulation of drugs in India are:

- Drugs and Cosmetics Act 1940 and its rules 1945
- Narcotic Drugs and Psychotropic Substances -1985
- Drugs Price Control Order 1995
- Consumer Protection Act-1986
- Factories Act-1948
- Law of Contracts (Indian contract Act-1872)
- Monopolistic & Restrictive Trade Practices Act-1969
- ICH GCP Guidelines
- Schedule Y Guidelines
- ICMR Guidelines
- Registry of Trial

Stages of approval-

1. Submission of Clinical Trial application for evaluating safety and efficacy.
2. Requirements for permission of new drugs approval.
3. Post approval changes in biological products: quality, safety and efficacy documents.
4. Preparation of the quality information for drug submission for new drug approval.

1. Submission of Clinical Trial Application for Evaluating Safety and Efficacy:

All the data listed below has to be produced.

a. Phase-I & phase- II clinical trial:

I. General information

- Introduction about company: Brief description about company

- Administrative headquarters: Provide address of company headquarters
- Manufacturing Facilities: Provide address of company headquarters
- Regulatory and intellectual property status in other countries.
- Patent information status in India & other countries

II. Chemistry manufacturing control

- Product Description: A brief description of the drug and the therapeutic class to which it belongs.
- Product Development
- Strain details
- Information on drug substance
- Information on drug Product

III. Non-clinical data: References: schedule – Y, amendment version 2005, Drugs and Cosmetics Rules, 1945

IV. Proposed phase-I / II studies: protocol for phase-I / II studies

b. Phase-III clinical trial:

All the information is as same as phase-I & phase- II clinical trial

- General information
- Chemistry manufacturing control
- Non-clinical data
- Proposed phase-III studies

2. Requirements for permission of New Drugs Approval

The manufacturer / sponsor have to submit application on Form 44 for permission of New Drugs Approval under the provisions of Drugs and Cosmetic Act 1940 and Rules 1945. The document design is as per the International submission requirements of Common Technical Document (CTD) and has five Modules.

Module I: Administrative/Legal Information

This module should contain documents specific to each region; for example, application forms or the proposed label for use in the region. The content and format of this module can be specified by the relevant regulatory authorities.

Module II: Summaries

Module 2 should begin with a general introduction to the pharmaceutical, including its pharmacologic class, mode of action and proposed clinical use. In general, the introduction should not exceed one page. The introduction should include proprietary name, nonproprietary name or common name of the drug substance, company name, dosage form(s), strength(s), route of administration, and proposed indication(s). It contains the CTD summaries for quality, safety, efficacy information. This module is very important, as it provides detailed summaries of the various sections of the CTD. These include: A very short introduction. Quality overall summary, Non clinical overview, Clinical over view, Non clinical written and tabulated summaries for pharmacology, pharmacokinetics, and toxicology.

Module III: Quality information (Chemical, pharmaceutical and biological)

Information on quality should be presented in the structured format described in the guidance M4Q. This document is intended to provide guidance on the format of a registration application for drug substances and their corresponding drug products. It contains of all of the quality documents for the chemistry, manufacture, and controls of the drug substance and the drug product.

Module IV: Non-clinical information

Information on safety should be presented in the structured format described in the guidance M4S. The purpose of this section is to present a critical analysis of the non-clinical data

pertinent to the safety of the medicinal product in the intended population. The analysis should consider all relevant data, whether positive or negative, and should explain why and how the data support the proposed indication and prescribing information. It gives final copy of all of the final nonclinical study reports.

Module V: Clinical information

Information on efficacy should be presented in the structured format described in the guidance M4E. It gives clinical summary including biopharmaceutics, pharmacokinetics and pharmacodynamics, clinical pharmacology studies, clinical efficacy, clinical safety, synopses of the individual studies and final copy of detailed clinical study reports.

3. Preparation of the quality information for drug submission for new drug approval

1. Drug substance (name, manufacturer)

2. Characterization (name, manufacturer)

    - Physicochemical characterization
    - Biological characterization

3. Drug product (name, dosage form)

4. Control of drug product (name, dosage form)

5. Appendices

    - Facilities and equipment (name, manufacturer)
    - Safety evaluation adventitious agents (name, dosage form, manufacturer).

Fees for Clinical Trial/Approval of New Drugs

- Phase I (IND) -Rs. 50000

- Phase II (IND) -Rs.25000

- Phase III(IND) -Rs.25000

- Approval of New Molecule -Rs.50000

- Approved New Drug: Within 1 Yr of approval -Rs.50000 After 1yr of approval -Rs.15000

- Approval of New claim, New Dosage form etc.Rs.15000.

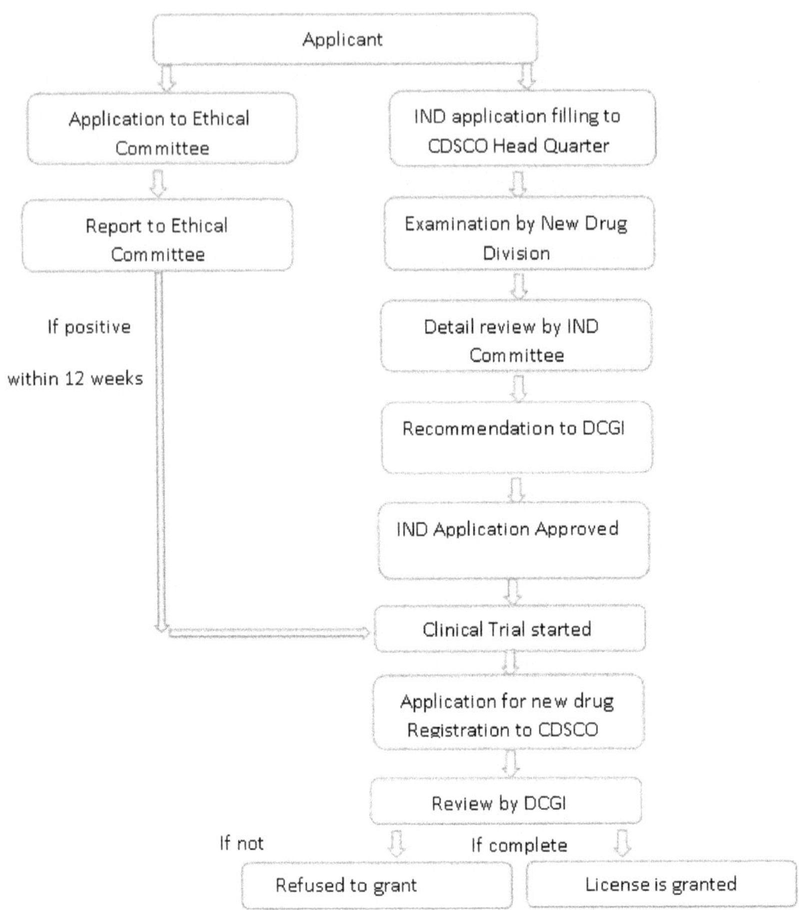

Drug Approval process in India

www.ingramcontent.com/pod-product-compliance
Ingram Content Group UK Ltd.
Pitfield, Milton Keynes, MK11 3LW, UK
UKHW021913190726
13853UKWH00002B/644